Rising After the Fall

From
UNTOLD NARRATIVES

With an Introduction by Lucy Hannah
and a foreword by Pashtana Durrani

Illustrated by
SARA RAHMANI

SCHOLASTIC

Edited by Lucy Hannah and Zarghuna Kargar, from a collective diary written by: Zainab Akhlaqi, Marie Bamyani, Freshta Ghani, Naeema Ghani, Batool Haidari, Fatema Haidari, Elahe Hosseini, Masouma Kawsari, Fatema Key, Maryam Mahjoba, Atifa Mozzaffari, Maliha Naji, Anahita Gharib Nawaz, Parand, Sharifa Pasun, Fatima Saadat, Farangis Elyassi Saboor and Rana Zurmaty

Published in the UK by Scholastic, 2023
1 London Bridge, London, SE1 9BG

Scholastic Ireland, 89E Lagan Road, Dublin Industrial Estate, Glasnevin, Dublin, D11 HP5F

SCHOLASTIC and associated logos are trademarks and/or
registered trademarks of Scholastic Inc.

ISBN 978 07023 2312 6

A CIP catalogue record for this book is available from the British Library.

A CIP catalogue record for this book is available from the British Library.

Printed in China by C&C Offset Printing Co., Ltd.
Paper made from wood grown in sustainable forests and other controlled sources.

1 3 5 7 9 10 8 6 4 2

www.scholastic.co.uk

Contents

Foreword

BY PASHTANA DURRANI

As I sit down to write this foreword for a group of Afghan women writers that hold a special place in my heart, I am reminded of the long summer days of 2021. It was during that time that I had the privilege of collaborating with these women, translating for them as they worked with Untold Narratives in the UK to develop their creative writing. I remember how each writer passionately defended the characters in their short stories, striving to create an authentic representation of life in Afghanistan.

As a well-known women's rights activist, I was at risk when the Taliban took over Afghanistan in August 2021. I managed to make my way out of the country, as this group of writers began to share their experiences of what was going on around them in a collective diary. They were driven by a need to stay connected to each other as their country collapsed around them.

The diary excerpts that make up *Rising After the Fall* remind me of the resilient Afghan women I grew up with. Too often, the international

media portrays Afghan women as victims, but the exchanges in this book show how different that portrayal is from the women I know.

As a child, I did not have access to children's literature that explored life in Afghanistan. Instead, I learned about our history and culture through the oral stories passed down to me from my mother and my grandmother. But now, in this book, young readers will have a chance to read about life in Afghanistan from these women's perspectives at a critical point in the country's history.

It is impossible to ignore the stark reality that Afghan women continue to face. The harsh truth is that Afghan women are still struggling to gain the basic rights and freedoms that we often take for granted. How much more suffering does there need to be before the world realizes this? Women of Afghanistan don't need rescuing, but they do need support. They deserve to breathe fresh air, dress as they choose and pursue their ambitions – they deserve to be able to live and think as they wish.

As I write this, it has been more than five hundred days since girls were last able to attend school in Afghanistan. I can't help but imagine how many of them may have been beaten and forced into marriage and how many of them may have had dreams of becoming writers – writers whose stories would connect young girls like me to their roots. And I hope that one day we will be able to pick up a book about Afghanistan without fear of being heartbroken, and instead find stories that reflect the beauty and intricacy of our lives.

I am grateful for the writers who contributed to this diary, as they have given voice to the many women of Afghanistan. Their words remind us of the importance of creative expression, particularly in a time of crisis. I hope that readers will be as inspired and moved by these brave women writers as I have been. I hope that this book will inspire others to share their own stories, and to find joy and hope in the midst of hardship.

Introduction

BY LUCY HANNAH

On 15 August 2021 (24 Asad 1400), Kabul, the capital city of Afghanistan, was retaken by the Taliban. A group of Afghan women writers realized that everything in their lives was about to change. As the world around them crumbled, they shared their thoughts, feelings and experiences with each other via a secure messaging app. The following messages from Nadia, Shekiba, Sola, Mariam, Amina, Fatima and Samira take us inside the minds of these women as the Taliban retook Afghanistan.

The Taliban is a religious group made up of the different tribes of Afghanistan. They believe in their own version of Islamic Sharia law and they impose strict rules about what women can and cannot do. When the Taliban entered Kabul, we at Untold Narratives were working with a group of Afghan women writers on their short stories to be published as a collection in English, translated from two of their first languages – Pashto and Dari. These are the two official languages of Afghanistan, and the most common among the forty or so that are spoken. The women writers were upset and alarmed as the Taliban swept across the whole of Afghanistan. They had ruled the country once before, between 1996 and 2001 (1375 and 1380); Shekiba and Samira, two of the older women, remembered those days and didn't want to return to them.

They worried for each other's safety, and they were scared that the

Taliban might stop girls from going to school, as they had done in the past. Also, a lot of Afghan men didn't think women should be writing anyway, so they needed to stick together.

The women had been sharing stories with each other online for more than two years. Despite coming from a range of ethnic groups and living in different parts of the country – Fatima was in Mazar-e-Sharif, 300 miles from Nadia in Herat – they were determined to stay connected. Friends are important, particularly when everything is changing around you, and the writers knew this was going to be a challenging time, so they began to exchange messages of support and encouragement daily, via a mobile phone app. As it grew, it came to be known as their collective 'diary'.

The writers responded to the Taliban in different ways. Nadia and Shekiba felt defiant and protested on the streets to support women's rights. Some decided to leave the country to find a better future where it is easier for women to live and work freely. Sola was given the chance to do this by her German employers, but that meant saying goodbye to her family, while Mariam chose a much riskier route out, paying smugglers to help her leave.

Several of these women felt threatened because of their ethnicity. Amina is Hazara, and historically they are a minority tribe who feel they haven't had equal rights with other people. Also, those whose family had worked with the Afghan army, like Fatima, felt at risk because they had been working against the Taliban.

The women contributed regularly to this virtual, collective, real-time diary for twelve months following the fall of Kabul. The excerpts that make up *Rising After the Fall* help us understand what it was like when the Taliban retook Afghanistan and what happened immediately after. The writers' names have been changed, but the spirit and courage of the real women behind their own words will always remain.

While reading the book you might come across some words or phrases that you've never heard of before. You can turn to the glossary at the back of the book to find out what they mean.

The Characters in this Book

Amina (64, Hazara)
is a grandmother with a large family.
She lives in Kabul.

Shekiba (53, Tajik)
works in the media, creating radio
programmes. She lives in Kabul,
with a large extended family, and
remembers the last time the Taliban
ruled Afghanistan 20 years ago.

Nadia (24, Tajik)
is a university student and activist.
She lives in Herat with her sister who
has a disability.

Sola (30, Pashtun)
works for a German NGO. She lives
with her parents and siblings in
Kabul, but moves to a small town in
Germany as a refugee.

Fatima (38, Uzbek)
is a journalist whose family all
worked for the Afghan army. She
finds her way to Tajikistan from
Mazar-e-Sharif, but she's not happy
there and wants to get to Europe
or America.

Mariam (36, Tajik)
escapes Afghanistan via unofficial
channels and is now living in Sweden
as a writer.

Samira (47, Uzbek)
is a teacher in Kabul. She is the main
breadwinner in her family.

KAZAKSTAN

UZBEKISTAN

KYRGYZSTAN

TAJIKISTAN

TURKMENISTAN

JOWZJAN
BALKH
KUNDUZ
BADAKHSHAN
TAKHAR

FARYAB
SAMANGAN
BAGHLAN

SAR-E POL

BADGHIS
BAMYAN
PANJSHIR
NURISTAN
KAPISA
PARWAN
KUNAR
LAGHMAN

HERAT
GHOR
WARDAK
KABUL ★
NANGARHAR

DAYKUNDI
LOGAR

PAKTIA
KHOST

GHAZNI

FARAH
URUZGAN

ZABUL
PAKTIKA

PAKISTAN

NIMROZ
KANDAHAR

HELMAND

A Map of
Afghanistan

Shock:
The Taliban Enter Kabul

In April 2021 (Hamal 1400), the US and allied troops announced they were leaving Afghanistan. They had been there for twenty years. During June, July and August, the Taliban made their way across the country, and on 15 August they entered the capital, Kabul. A group of writers who had been working together used a secure messaging app to stay connected – seven of them share their story here.

15th August 2021

Shekiba

The Taliban have reached Kota-e-Sangi just west of Kabul. Phone connections are bad, the internet barely works. I really hope we don't lose our connection. I hope all of you are OK. Please let me know how you are and where you are. I'm at home, but worried sick.

07:59

Fatima

The Taliban have entered our area, they are everywhere. They say, we won't say anything to you girls, as long as you obey the Islamic dress code. Are you all OK?

08:08

Mariam

Oh my God, it's true, they've come.

08:10

Fatima

They entered the city so quietly, I hope it isn't the calm before the storm. The best thing some people did was to leave the country before all this happened.

08:16

Mariam

From our experience, in the first few days they're very quiet, but as time passes, they start enforcing their unfair rules on innocent people.

08:21

HISTORY OF THE TALIBAN IN AFGHANISTAN

In 1979, the Soviet Union invaded Afghanistan, starting a war that lasted ten years. Many Afghans, especially those with strong religious beliefs, were unhappy with the situation and started leaving the country. Some took refuge in Pakistan and were supported by the United States (US) in the fight against the Afghan government, which was backed by the Soviets. These religious groups were called the Mujahideen, and in 1992 they took over Afghanistan. In 1994, after a civil war erupted among different ethnic groups of the Mujahideen, a small group of students in the province of Kandahar in southern Afghanistan formed a new group called the Taliban.

In 1996, the Taliban took over Kandahar. Soon they controlled most of the country and set up a new government. The Taliban's rule was harsh as they instituted a strict version of Islamic law. When al-Qaeda, a terrorist group led by Osama bin Laden, attacked and destroyed the World Trade Center in New York in 2001, the Taliban gave refuge to Osama bin Laden and refused to give him up. The US and the United Kingdom (UK) declared war and invaded Afghanistan, taking much of the land that the Taliban had claimed. Although many of their leaders were

killed, the Taliban didn't go away, and they slowly began fighting the US-backed Afghan government and seizing some areas of Afghanistan.

In August 2021, around the time the US and the UK were withdrawing troops from Afghanistan, the Taliban launched a new attack, overrunning the country within weeks before finally storming Kabul, the capital city. The Afghan government's army collapsed, and the Taliban took over Afghanistan once more.

Shekiba

I hear in Herat they've stopped women from going to university.

08:21

Nadia

I don't think I'll be able to go to study again. Here in Herat, they've taken over the city, there is some fighting, women are not allowed to work, and they've closed down universities and schools for girls. All the government offices have been evacuated.

08:22

Amina

We might also be under threat here in Kabul. I heard that the Taliban have threatened a famous poet and writer, so they might be after other writers and social activists. I'm scared.

08:32

Fatima

I'm really frightened too, the Taliban are searching house after house. I really hope they don't come to ours. My family has been working with the army. My brother was killed fighting as a soldier. My parents are also army officers and so is my sister. If they find out, it could be very dangerous for us.

08:36

Amina

Are the Taliban searching all the houses – I mean every single house?

08:36

Sola

Please don't be scared. Someone reported our house, saying it's the home of an army officer and that we might have weapons. The Taliban came and searched, but they couldn't find anything, so they left.

08:37

WHY ARE THE AFGHAN ARMED FORCES FRIGHTENED?

In the 1994–96 war, after the Taliban captured a province, they would search the area and arrest government officials and soldiers, sometimes executing them. When Kabul fell in 2021, the Taliban again began arresting soldiers and anyone they thought had worked for the government. Hundreds of people disappeared during this time, and it's likely that many of them were killed. Some people in positions of power managed to escape the country as the Taliban retook Kabul, but lots of army and police officers had to fend for themselves as they tried to hide their past or leave the country.

Amina

I'm still scared about our books and our writing. I'm frightened they might do something to them.

08:37

Sola

They haven't said anything about books. They won't touch them. Don't worry!

08:37

THE TALIBAN'S VIEW ON GIRLS' EDUCATION

The Taliban have a history of suppressing girls' education. Some members of the Taliban still believe that girls don't need to go to school because of their gender. When the Taliban first came to power in 1996, they closed all girls' schools and stopped women from attending university. However, when the Taliban took over Afghanistan for the second time, in 2021, they promised equal rights for women and men. People were hopeful that they might have changed their strict attitude. After the takeover, however, they announced that girls could only attend primary school.

Nadia

So, what do they want? Only God knows. We certainly don't. My sister and I are members of a social activist group. People will know that we wanted to speak to some mullahs about girls' education. I don't know what will happen now.

08:38

MULLAHS

Muslims go to mosques to perform their prayers. Each mosque is led by a local leader called a *mullah*. Mullahs usually join a madrasah (religious school) to learn about Islamic law and how to lead the community in prayer.

Amina

Those of you who are in Kabul, please stay safe, do not leave your homes. I hope nothing will happen to Kabul and its people. People say the Taliban will be speaking from the presidential palace soon and we'll hear what's happening.

08:54

Shekiba

I hope and pray that civilians don't suffer because of the Taliban's hunger for power.

08:59

Samira

Don't worry, my dear, it's just a transition period. We must not lose hope and determination. We should not believe any propaganda or fake news.

09:00

WHAT IS 'FAKE NEWS'?

Fake news is a term that refers to a news story or image that has been deliberately made up in order to make people believe something that isn't true. After the Taliban victory in 2021, pictures appeared online of refugees holding weapons. However, the weapons had been added to the images digitally to make the refugees look like terrorists. Sometimes, people call stories which are true 'fake news' to convince other people to disbelieve them.

Mariam

Dear Samira, no matter who is fighting who, it's ordinary Afghans who will suffer the most. The Taliban are wild, they will never learn lessons from the past.

09:04

Shekiba

Unfortunately, that's true. I went to my office, and I was told that the situation is getting worse, and you have to go home. I didn't feel any fear because it felt the same as events twenty-six years ago, but for the sake of my two colleagues who are younger than me, I had to leave. They looked panicked. The city was crowded, and chaos spread. All the people were in a frenzy, and a man came and told the driver of our office car, 'Brother, leave the women and run away. You need to think about yourself – leave the job.' So, we went and took a taxi, but that driver also had a phone call from his office telling him to leave us and save his car. My jaw dropped – I felt that these men had changed suddenly. I asked myself, is it really only the Taliban who are against women's freedom, or all of my countrymen? We three women were just abandoned in the crowd. Some of the men made fun of us. They were saying, 'You women will be trapped at home from tomorrow.' Some even tried to physically and verbally harass us. We walked for two hours to reach our homes.

09:10

20

Fatima

This morning the Taliban had a gathering in our part of Mazar-e-Sharif. They were roaming around, we could actually see them. People were in shock. I was so scared. We all left our offices early, and it took me six hours to get home. Normally it takes an hour. I felt that every Talib fighter I passed on the street might start shooting at me. It was terrifying.

12:56

Samira

For me, my day started as usual at school. I passed out exam papers to my students and gave them instructions. I explained the procedure to them. The class was calm and quiet. Then our headteacher burst in. His hands were shaking and he was in dismay. My heart started pounding. I had been worried all the previous night. I knew something was going to happen. I started collecting the unfinished papers from my students – they were all scared, and some had turned pale. The headteacher and I told the students to leave as soon as possible.

The streets were crowded, and it was difficult to get home. None of the pedestrians and cyclists were giving way to one another. There was panic and horror, roads were blocked, and no one knew what was happening. I decided to try a different route, but luckily at that moment my brother had come to find me in his car and picked me up. I was a bit shaken but not as shocked as some. It isn't the first time I've experienced such chaos. I feel used to this kind of instability. What makes me really sad is that I spent my childhood at war and as a young woman, and I'm now experiencing it again. I feel like war never leaves me.

13:10

AFGHANISTAN'S UNSTABLE PAST

Since its formation in the 1760s, the area we now know as Afghanistan was first ruled by Ahmad Shah Durrani. He became leader by conquering and uniting all the different tribes, establishing Afghanistan as a country. However, the peace didn't last as Afghanistan had to fight off invasions by British forces in 1839 and 1878.

In 1901, Afghanistan became more stable under the rule of King Habibullah Khan. However, many years of conflict had left most of the power in the country with tribal leaders. In 1973, Afghanistan's monarchy was overthrown, and the country became a republic, but there was still instability across the country. A new government was set up by Hafizullah Amin. Amin's government allied with the Soviet Union and tried to change things, but many religious people disliked this and began a rebellion against the government. The rebellion ended in 1989. In 1994, the Taliban was formed by a small group of religious students who wanted to restore what they deemed the correct religious belief in Afghanistan.

Mariam

We needed some cash, but the bank is far away from where I live. I walked through the market, where men and women were busy shopping for their groceries. For a moment, I felt happy that life was going on as normal. I saw some people from our neighbourhood and high school girls in their black uniforms with white headscarves. When I arrived at the bank, there was a huge crowd. I thought there was a protest – people were shouting and swearing at the bank staff, and one person had already started a fight. The police were trying to bring some order. I was terrified and decided to go back home.

In the blink of an eye, the calmness in the market changed to chaos and people were running. Many shops closed suddenly, and I could hear people saying that the Taliban had passed the Pul-e-Charkhi prison and had entered the city from all four sides. They had broken down the prison doors and let the prisoners loose. The streets were emptying as men on motorbikes passed by with guns in their hands. They had long, dirty hair. These were the scenes I had seen on TV, now I was seeing them with my own eyes. There was gunfire and planes overhead, but after a while the shooting stopped. Then I heard the news: Ashraf Ghani, the president, had left the country with his assistants and the Taliban had taken control of the presidential palace.

14:03

WHO IS ASHRAF GHANI?

Ashraf Ghani was born in 1949 in the province of Logar in eastern Afghanistan. In 1974, he went to the US to study and became a professor of anthropology (the study of how human societies develop) and worked for the World Bank. Ghani returned to Afghanistan in 2002,

with the aim of helping his country after the first Taliban government was thrown out. He first worked as finance minister, and then in 2004 he became an adviser to the government and developed projects to help the country get back on its feet once the US and UK troops left Afghanistan.

In 2014, Ghani became the president and promised to rebuild the country. He was re-elected in 2020, but after Kabul fell to the Taliban in August 2021, he escaped to the United Arab Emirates.

Amina

I feel helpless. Our president has sold out our homeland and escaped. My country has no leader. He's left us alone to suffer. I don't know how to digest what's happening. I'm writing through my pain. I weep for my country. I weep for the proud soldiers who fought in the battleground, I weep for the mothers who worry for their young daughters. My tears won't stop, they flow like a river. I want to fly high, high to the top of the Hindu Kush mountains. I want to scream the pain of my country out loud. I want to scream so loud that even the Deaf can hear it.

17:40

16ᵗʰ August 2021

Nadia

Visiting relatives has always been my favourite thing to do in Herat. I love going out, but when my father asked me to go to my uncle's house for safety last night, I felt a great darkness and sadness. I'm anxious, and I remembered the day when my brother, who was a soldier, got killed in a battle with the Taliban. I couldn't imagine that one day those who murdered my brother would take over our city. But we must not lose hope, I refuse to go back in time. None of us will allow darkness to come. Our people's dream of having a peaceful country will come true very soon.

08:31

Shekiba

This morning, in Kabul, I heard the call for prayer from the mosque's loudspeakers. I prayed and tried to listen to the birds singing, but I couldn't hear them. You won't believe me, but it's true. The whole city is silent. I saw dogs, but they weren't barking, it seemed as though they were scared too. Now I don't hear any aeroplanes. I hid behind the curtains. I saw the Taliban walking and shouting on the streets, saying: 'Search him!' I'm at home now. I can hear gunfire. No one comes out of their homes. I ask God to protect the young women of my country. They should not become the victims of forced marriages and abuse. I just heard a big explosion. I'm terrified.

10:34

DIFFERENT CALENDARS

Most parts of the world use the Common Era (CE) system in which there are 365 days in a year and the first year (1 CE) corresponds to 1 AD — the year Jesus Christ is thought to have been born. But in most Islamic countries, the calendar (Solar Hijri Calendar) starts at the Hegira — the time when the Prophet Muhammad emigrated from Mecca to the town of Medina, in Saudi Arabia, in 622 CE. This year is called 1 AH. As the Islamic months coincide with the phases of the moon, the Islamic year has 354 or 355 days (rather than 365). This means that each year passes slightly quicker than in the Common Era. For example, in 2022 CE, the Islamic year was 1444 AH.

In countries where there are many Shia Muslims, such as Iran, a slightly different calendar is used. This also begins at 1 AH, but the year has 365 days. It is called the Jalali calendar, and 2022 is 1401 in the Jalali system.

Amina

The changes these days remind me of the years 1376–77 (1997–98). The same fear, the same silence, and now after twenty years the same thing is happening – history repeats itself in front of my eyes. Sometimes I think that Afghanistan is the end of the world, where the sky and earth are stuck together. Here everything happens so fast. The only thing that doesn't change is people's attitude. Those difficult days of my life were like today's dark days. In 1376 (1997), I remember writing a story to empty the burden from my heart. I read my story when I was visiting a gathering of the writer's association of Balkh province. The event was broadcast by our local TV channel. The next day the Taliban took over Mazar-e-Sharif. Here's my story from back then:

12:19

Like Water

The sun was setting and the heat from its rays was cooling. My mother was right: when you're ill, before you get better you feel the worst pain. My bones are aching, my cough is not stopping. I came to the area where the bread was being baked, and I sat. I feel suffocated. The silence is scary. I can only hear gunfire. The people around me want to identify the sounds of bombs and rockets.

Sometimes we hear the neighbour's dog barking. The dog sounds so disturbed. I haven't heard the noise of kids playing outside. I hope they're in their homes and haven't gone anywhere; this silence is not due to loneliness, so I'm wondering what it is. I don't want to remind myself that this is the silence of fear. When there's gunfire and the electricity is cut, a strange quiet takes over. I can hear my mother combing the carpet she's weaving to remove loose threads. When I listen to her weaving, I feel hopeful. I don't know why.

The lady from next door peeks over the yard's wall. She gulps and says the Taliban have entered the city. What is going to happen now? My mum looks up towards the sky, knocks on the wall and says, 'God forbid, I hope that day never comes.' The lady says they showed the Taliban on the TV a few days ago.

I ask her, 'Auntie, what are the Taliban like?'

She says, 'Oh, my dear, I hope you never see them. They have long beards, big turbans and dirty clothes. Some of them don't even wear shoes.'

I felt I knew the Taliban; I knew they were scary. They remind me of a memory from long ago: I woke up in the middle of the night to the shouting of my father; he was beating my mother. I could only see his shadow on the wall from under the duvet. I feared him. He also had a long

beard and wore a white turban; he looked like a Talib to me.

The next-door lady says, 'The Taliban say women should not go outside, girls should not go to school, and they should not wear colourful clothes. They must wear burqas.'

The cough does not go away, and when it does, my shoulders and all my bones ache.

I don't like staying indoors. I go to the window. I feel very weak. I lean my head against the glass. I hear gunfire and my mother is still combing the threads of the carpet. I also combed the thread of the carpets until a year ago, but since I've been ill, I haven't been able to weave anymore. When I was weaving the carpets, I thought I was weaving the moments of my life with the thread.

My mother has sold the only white clothes she had; she hasn't been wearing them for a while. We don't work outside the house, we don't study now; if we go out, we wear a big chador.

I lift my head from the stained glass. I only remember writing my name when I went to school. I try to write it on the window, which has steamed up. As I write my name the vapour melts on the glass and slips off of it. My name disappears with it.

Fatima

Thank you for sharing your story, Amina. My head is bursting with pain, but I'm trying to stay positive. I want to believe that everything will be fine, but I hear gunfire, and with each shot I feel my heart stop. What if the Taliban really do start searching our homes? My family and I will be the first ones to pay the price for working with foreigners. My heart is full of sorrow. I'm sad. Today is the darkest day of my life. What will tomorrow be like?

16:49

Chaos:
The Scramble to Escape

Just days before the Taliban took control of Afghanistan's capital, Kabul, the US, the UK, Canada and others started evacuating thousands of their employees and eligible Afghans to other countries. The evacuation from Kabul airport ended on 30 August along with the full withdrawal of the US military. This was the end of twenty years of occupation of Afghanistan by the US. While some local Afghans were evacuated, some tried but were not able to leave and others chose to stay. The writers wondered whether to stay or to go, discussing their options and supporting each other through their messages.

20ᵗʰ August 2021

Amina

Everyone is leaving. I'm scared – I have nowhere to go. How do you find the courage to leave? The world's news headlines are full of events at Kabul airport. Everyone's talking about what's happening to Afghans. Some people were making fun of this situation on social media. It made me angry and I felt I had to comment on one post, so I said, 'You're not in this situation, it's unfair to make fun of us and our desperation.' Everyone knows that clinging on to a flying plane means certain death. But very few understand that this was an act of protest against the betrayal of a nation.

12:32

WHAT HAPPENED AT KABUL AIRPORT

In the days after Kabul fell, the Taliban let foreign countries evacuate their citizens and the people who had worked with them. Thousands of people who wanted to leave arrived at the airport, but there weren't enough planes to take all of them. One American C-17 military transport plane designed for 150 passengers took over 600 evacuees from Kabul Airport.

People were so desperate that some stormed the airport runways to try to force their way on to flights. Some even tried to hold on to the airplane's undercarriages as they took off. One American C-17 plane took off with at least four people clinging to it. Unfortunately, these acts of sheer desperation ended in tragedy as these passengers were unable to hold on.

Fatima

I agree. Whenever I see the pictures of my people struggling to get to the airport and the plight of that young Afghan clinging on to the plane, it feels like the beginning of the fall of our country. As I see it, that man, Zaki Anwari, was not one person – he was the symbol of the Afghan nation, a nation he thought had escaped in 2001 with the fall of the Taliban government. And clinging on to that aeroplane, that modern technology, he found himself climbing through the sky towards hope. Now, in 2021, he will fall to the ground again from the same sky. This is an anxious and fragmented nation, where people want to touch the wing of every iron bird.

17:57

22nd August 2021

Mariam

Today there are 640 people sitting close to each other, ready to escape from Afghanistan. They are a pile of humans in a cold military plane; you can see people sitting almost on top of each other as there is not enough space for all of them. This is our geography and our reality; our people are the poorest of the poor. These people are struggling to fit in these aeroplanes because they don't want to die in their own land. These are the ones who worked hard, they made progress in education, learned skills, moved forward in life. They had dreams for a future. They had vision, and now their only hope is to fit in this big metal box in order to find freedom. The young man holding on to the wing of the flying plane was a footballer – and not just any footballer. He was Zaki Anwari, a nineteen-year-old who played for Afghanistan's national youth team. Sadly, he died in his bid for freedom and happiness.

09:30

23rd August 2021

Mariam

Dear friends, do you have any plans to go?

04:45

Nadia

What kind of plan do you mean?

05:00

Shekiba

A plan to leave Afghanistan and go to another country.

05:01

HOW EASY WAS IT FOR AFGHANS TO LEAVE THE COUNTRY?

Normally if a person wishes to leave their country, they need a passport and sometimes a visa to enter a different country. After Kabul fell, all the government offices and foreign consulates closed, and it was almost impossible to get a passport or apply for a visa. Even people who had passports and visas couldn't leave because the Taliban controlled access to the airports, eventually closing them after the evacuation. Some countries arranged special flights for their citizens and Afghans who had worked for them. In a panic and due to fear of the Taliban, hundreds of

ordinary Afghans went to the airport in the hope that a Western country might help them escape. The entrance to the airport was so packed it became very dangerous, and once people arrived, if they didn't have the correct papers they were not allowed on to the planes. Many people didn't have the money to give to the smugglers who offered to help people escape through neighbouring countries — for example, many went to Iran. Others stayed in Afghanistan because they thought the change of government wouldn't affect them.

WHAT IS A VISA?

A visa is a document which gives someone the right to visit another country as a tourist or to live or work there. People normally apply for a visa in their home country at the embassy of the country they wish to go to. Some countries have agreements with each other to allow their citizens to visit the other without a visa, but in some countries such as Afghanistan, citizens need visas to go to almost any other country.

Fatima

For the last few years, my siblings have suggested we leave Afghanistan and go somewhere safer. But my parents and I didn't want to flee because we know the bitter truth of becoming a refugee far from home. But looking at what is happening now, I feel we have made a big mistake by staying. Do you know anything about the buses which are taking people from the hotels to the airport – for those who are being evacuated?

23:10

Shekiba

Yes, people who have got hold of a visa are being transferred by buses. Have you received any emails regarding the evacuation? Only people who have the email invite and a visa are allowed to go.

23:42

Mariam

Oh, lucky them! It means they won't be waiting in the queues. I heard that there have been armed clashes at the airport. Is that true?

23:43

Shekiba

Yes, I heard that too, and they say there was fighting. I've been so worried I can't sleep.

23:45

Samira

I can't sleep either. The US is flying above my head. Where are we? I can't focus on anything. I don't know what to make of this situation. Why did all this happen? I don't know, I can't think of a reason. The government we had was elected by the people, but no one protected it. Why won't the noise of the military planes stop? History will remember all this.

23:45

Nadia

Oh God, I thought it was only me who couldn't sleep because of worry and concern for my land and my people.

23:54

Mariam

I hear some people are taken straight away without queuing or waiting; those people are in a very special category. I worry about my daughter. Do you know where these helicopters are taking people to? Are they there to help people evacuate?

23:55

WHO DECIDED WHO COULD LEAVE AND WHO COULD STAY?

• •

Even with a passport, it became very difficult to leave the country as the foreign officials who would usually issue visas had fled Afghanistan, which made applying almost impossible. Foreign governments set up special schemes to issue visas to Afghan refugees and people who they had worked with and those at risk of persecution from the Taliban. Organizations like the United Nations High Commission for Refugees tried to help, but there were just too many refugees, which meant many people left Afghanistan overland without the correct documents, or had no choice but to stay behind.

25ᵗʰ August 2021

Shekiba
Some people spent five days at the entrance to the airport. They only managed to go in after all that time. These were people who had all the necessary documents.

10:23

Fatima
Documents such as visas and passports?

11:24

41

Shekiba

Yes, they must have them.

12:24

Samira

I wish I had a visa, but my family and I are stuck here in Kabul and can't move or go anywhere.

12:52

Sola

It must be very hard. It feels like Judgement Day. I can't believe what is happening.

23:43

26th August 2021

Amina

The Taliban won't allow anyone to enter the airport. The Pakistani officials at the border won't allow Afghans in. There are rumours that after the US forces leave, there will be a Hazara genocide. I'm very worried.

My sister said a young man from our neighbourhood got into an argument with the security guards at the airport then a few armed men started beating him. She told me the story with tears in her eyes. She also said we don't have peace in our country and that she's heartbroken. I know the kind of pain she's going through. We've suffered this pain for many years. I couldn't

calm her down, I didn't know what to say. Suddenly, I exploded: 'Stop it, sister! Why do you take people's words so seriously? Not everything people say is true!' She went silent, and I started crying. I cried for all the misery and loneliness of my people.

09:49

AFGHANISTAN'S ETHNIC GROUPS

Afghanistan is made up of different ethnic groups:

- The biggest group are the **PASHTUN**, who live across Afghanistan and speak Pashtu.
- The next largest group are the **TAJIKS**, who primarily live in the north and northeast and speak Dari.
- The third ethnic group are the **HAZARAS**, who live in central Afghanistan. They are a minority and are mostly Shia Muslims.
- The **UZBEKS** and **TURKMEN** live mainly in the north. They speak Uzbeki and Turkmeni, but most of them also speak Dari.
- The **AIMAQS** are nomads in the northwest of Afghanistan. They speak a dialect of Turkish mixed with Persian.
- The **BALUCHIS** live in the south, close to the Pakistani border.
- Other ethnic groups include the **PASHIAE**, **NURISTANI**, **QIZILBASH**, **GUJUR** and **KYRGYZ**.

Nadia
People are being evacuated from Mazar airport today.

09:50

Samira
Those are domestic flights with Kam Air. Every time I think about what's happening at the airport, it feels like the situation is going to get worse.

11:02

Shekiba
I'm hopeful. Let's think positive. There is a light after every dark night.

17:34

Fatima
Thank you, Shekiba, let's be each other's strength. I hope we all reach our destinations safely.

23:22

30th August 2021

Amina
Apart from black tea, I can't taste any food or drink. No colour is pleasant for me these days. No tree is like before. I haven't heard any birds for twelve days. The only thing which gives me comfort

now is to be with my family. Instead of reading books, I'm reading the news, and I read the same lines again and again. All I see are tired people shouting for their fundamental human rights and all I hear is the sound of aeroplanes, which have become part of my daily life.

We have all been left alone to die. When the foreign troops leave for good, the Taliban will do whatever they want. Has anyone from our group left the country yet?

12:45

Mariam

I don't know. It's not easy.

15:01

WHAT IS A HUMAN RIGHT?

Human rights are basic rights which belong to everyone, regardless of their race, sex or religion. Everyone is entitled to these rights from birth. In 1948, human rights were recorded in a document called the UN Declaration of Human Rights and signed by almost all countries around the world.

These rights include: the right to life and liberty, the forbidding of enslavement and torture, the right to a fair trial, the right to education, the right to marry, the right to claim asylum in another country, the right to vote in free elections and the right to freedom of thought and expression. The Taliban has been accused of breaching the UN Declaration of Human Rights.

Shekiba

Hello, does anyone know where the explosions and rocket firing were coming from?

15:48

Samira

Yes, dear, the attack was at 7 p.m. today. I heard that it was near Kabul airport. It hit a house, and people suspect that the US forces did it.

15:51

Amina

Yes, some kids were killed. It was very scary. Why should we trust the US? Everyone's playing political games and we are the dice.

16:02

NO ONE TO TRUST

When things change as fast as they did in Afghanistan, it's difficult for people to know who to trust — one misjudgement could lead to a person being arrested or worse. The US promised that everyone who had worked for them would be evacuated, but that wasn't possible before the last US flight left Kabul on 30 August 2021.

The Taliban promised not to persecute those who had worked for the old government or the Americans, but hundreds of those people were mistreated. The Taliban also promised to protect human rights, but they arrested protestors, banned marches and closed schools for girls. Many promises were made, only to be broken.

Samira

This was inevitable. But people kept going and the huge crowd at the gates just got bigger. The news does not surprise me because explosions are nothing new to Kabul. I just hope that there aren't too many casualties. I saw family members screaming and shouting trying to find their loved ones. It made me feel sick. I felt a headache coming on. I switched off the TV and closed down my social media accounts. The explosion still didn't stop people from going to the airport. Those who have managed to leave Afghanistan are considered heroes and those who are left behind are the unlucky ones, people say. Whenever I hear someone I know has fled, it makes me feel helpless and miserable. I say to myself, lucky them! We'll stay here and deal with the misery of life. As I lie on my bed I think about how this situation is just like a horror movie.

16:31

Shekiba

Friends, if you want to leave and can leave Afghanistan, it's best to do it as soon as possible. But you must have patience. I've been trying for three years to go abroad for medical treatment but I didn't manage it. Now we don't even have a government. So it's much harder.

17:11

Samira

It's very difficult. I hear the process of applying for asylum takes a long time.

17:15

WHAT IS 'SEEKING ASYLUM'?

People often seek asylum in other countries because they are being persecuted in their home country for their political or religious beliefs, their ethnicity or because their human rights have been violated. The process of asking permission to flee to another country is called seeking asylum. A government will often grant asylum if they believe the refugee's fear of persecution is genuine. In 2021, there were 4.6 million people seeking asylum around the world, many of them from Afghanistan.

Sola

Yes, now the situation is critical and the application process is slow. If I don't leave, the Taliban won't allow me to complete my education, and because I work with foreigners, my life may be at risk. My German colleagues may be able to help me.

17:18

Fatima

If we get the chance, why not? I will leave. We applied for asylum but never got a reply. If we want to apply through the UN refugee agency (UNHCR) to be settled in another country, we have to go to Tajikistan first, and that's not easy.

18:01

WHICH AFGHANS DID THE INTERNATIONAL COMMUNITY HELP AND WHY?

The US and NATO had soldiers stationed in Afghanistan. As Kabul was falling, these soldiers helped evacuate 120,000 people by air – primarily non-Afghan citizens and around 2,000 Afghans who had worked for NATO. Countries such as the UK had worked with many Afghans and tried to help them leave by air or by land. Unfortunately, many of these attempts failed and lots

of Afghans were left behind. Afghan soldiers, political leaders, women's rights activists and judges were also in danger and sought help to escape. Around 800,000 Afghans were forced from their homes by the fighting but remained in the country. They were offered food, aid and housing by the international community.

1ˢᵗ September 2021

Mariam

Today a girl shared this on her Facebook page and I read it. I need to share it.

> **Today during the airport chaos, a woman asked me to look after her child. I said maybe, but what if I lose you in this crowd and your child is left to me?! She cried and said, 'I am trying to rescue my other five children. I have no option. If we get separated, you just take her with you.'**

I've been thinking about that mother and the desperate situation she was in, trying hard to get her children to safety. I watched a short video of what was happening at Kabul airport. I watched how a father was stuck in the crowd and he had to hand his child over to an American soldier. People on social media were questioning how he could give his child to a stranger. But the reality is that he wants them to go to a safer place and have a brighter future.

09:31

Amina

I saw the image of a child who was at the entrance of the airport! I think about his mother, my heart aches for him. I want to understand better how or why they became separated. I feel this is the sacrifice of a mother: it doesn't matter how much she suffers, she just wants her child to have peace and a future.

09:41

Fatima

All I hear these days are these words and they make me feel furious:

'Canada is letting in twenty thousand refugees.'

'You are not on the evacuees list!'

'Do you have any Western friends who can help?'

'You are literate, so you will be able to go!'

'So and so went, why are you still here? If I were you I would have left by now.'

'Are you still in Mazar or have you left?'

Will these questions ever end?

09:50

Protest:
We Must Resist

After returning to power, the Taliban set about enforcing policies that limited women's and girls' access to education and healthcare, and their freedoms of movement and expression. Women were squeezed out of many government jobs, barred from travelling alone and ordered to dress according to a strict interpretation of the Quran. Shekiba and Nadia joined other women who responded by holding small protests where they demanded their right to education and work.

WHAT IS THE QURAN?

The Quran is the Muslim holy book. The Quran is divided into thirty parts and 114 surahs (or verses) of various lengths. Muslims believe the Quran was revealed to the Prophet Muhammad over a period of twenty-three years. Some people and stories appear in both the Quran and the Christian Bible, such as Musa (known as Moses in the Bible) and Nuh (known as Noah in the Bible) and the Flood.

17ᵗʰ August 2021

> **Fatima**
>
> Today I saw Afghan women protesting for their rights. Well done to these brave ladies! This shows how resilient we are.
>
> 19:34

20ᵗʰ August 2021

> **Shekiba**
>
> I touch my bracelet – the two sides of it are red and, in the middle, it has a white stripe. It reminds me of when I used to wear it during my protest against fraud in the presidential elections. I have also kept my purple scarf, which I used to wear during the Enlightenment protest. It was held by mainly the Hazara minority community, who demanded equal rights,

opportunities and protection from the attacks on Shia targets. Afghans around the country were protesting for security.

Our slogan was: 'Achieving success later is better than achieving nothing.' I also look at my ID card and the sticker on the back of my voting card for the elections. I still remember those days. These thoughts fill my head, and I can't think of anything else right now.

12:33

PROTESTING IN AFGHANISTAN

People protest by forming a group and calling for change. They often do this by gathering in public spaces to ask a government or organization to reform policies they believe need changing.

Queen Soraya was the wife of King Amanullah Khan. As queen, she played a big part in the women's freedom movement in the 1920s. She argued that women should not have to wear the burqa and should have the right to be educated. Afghan women talk about her proudly.

In 1996, the Taliban restricted women's rights by forcing them to wear hijabs (head coverings) and by ruling that they couldn't leave the house without a male guardian. Afghan women protested even though they risked being

arrested and beaten by Taliban fighters. In 2001, groups such as the Committee on Afghan Women's Political Participation rose to fight for the rights they had lost under oppression by the Taliban, and against new laws which might restrict them further.

THE ENLIGHTENMENT MOVEMENT

In 2016, a new power cable was laid from Turkmenistan into Afghanistan. But President Ghani's government decided to change the route of the cable so that it no longer ran through Bamiyan, a major Hazara province, and was moved to Salang, an area where many Tajiks live. The Hazara community, who have felt persecuted under the different regimes in the country, had hoped the new cable would provide jobs and improve conditions for them. As a result, many Hazara students and activists formed a group called the Enlightenment Movement and demanded that Ghani change his mind. When he didn't, they began to protest, and in May 2016 over a million people marched in Kabul. Islamic State (IS) suicide bombers attacked an Enlightenment Movement march in the same year and killed more than eighty people. Even though protests continued through online campaigns and rallies outside Afghanistan, the government kept the cable running through Salang.

Nadia

A while ago I heard the voice of a woman from the other side of the door. She was talking to her neighbours. She said, 'Look, sister! Don't worry, the Taliban won't say anything to women like you and me. We're not educated. We were wearing the burqa before and we will wear it now. We have nothing to worry about. These other women should be staying at home like me and you. That way they will be safe and the Taliban won't say anything to them.' I listened to her and I thought to myself, what is the difference between these women and me? I thought for a while, then I got up, got dressed, put on my red lipstick and decided to join the protests.

16:40

25th August 2021

Fatima

Freedom is greater than food, water and air, and we don't have it at the moment.

18:10

28th August 2021

Mariam

I still can't believe how fast we have accepted the Taliban, how quickly we are losing our human rights. I'm waiting to see what will happen.

11:29

THE TALIBAN'S VIEWS ON WOMEN'S CLOTHING AND HEAD COVERINGS

The Taliban's views on Islamic law are strict. They believe that the shape of a woman's body shouldn't be visible, so Afghan women must wear a hijab or a niqab (which covers the face, but not the eyes) or a type of burqa, which the Afghans themselves call a chadari.

A burqa is a cloak-like piece of clothing that covers a woman's body entirely. Burqas often have a mesh panel to cover the eyes, allowing the woman to see out. The Quran (the Muslim holy book) states a woman should wear modest clothes, but it doesn't say exactly what that clothing should be. Consequently, different Islamic groups throughout history have followed their own rules. In Afghanistan, women living in conservative areas may have chosen to wear a burqa, but when the Taliban took over, they ruled that when a woman leaves her house, she must be completely covered.

chadari/ burqa

niqab

hijab

Nadia

The Taliban have warned women not to go out to protest in Mazar. I really hope some media organizations notice us and report our demonstrations to the rest of the world. Do you have your slogans ready? I think if we have banners that say, 'Protest for women's rights', lots of people will join in. I think journalists and the media will be interested. If these groups attend, the protests will be more effective. If the media is there, the Taliban will not get violent.

08:18

WHY IS THE TALIBAN CONCERNED ABOUT ITS IMAGE?

The Taliban depends on financial aid from other countries. The old Afghan government received approximately three-quarters of its money through foreign aid, but if the Taliban behave in a way that other governments don't like, they may stop helping Afghanistan. For example, in 2021 the US froze more than $9 billion that belonged to the Afghan Central Bank because it objected to the Taliban's human rights violations. So far, no country has officially recognized the Taliban as legitimate rulers of Afghanistan. If this continues, the Taliban government won't be able to feed people or rebuild the hospitals and roads destroyed by the war.

Samira
The girls are heading towards Shahr-e-Naw. They will gather in the park.

08:46

Amina
Oh, I wish I'd known about this earlier. It's not easy for me to come and join the protest right now.

08:53

Nadia

Today I became the character in the book I'm writing. This is exactly how I imagined my character – I became myself! I wrote slogans and made banners for the protest, I spoke to people, I looked into the eyes of the Taliban and yelled for my freedom and demanded my rights. I saw one of them walking up and down the road like a hungry wolf. He was shouting and pointing his gun at us. I knew if his seniors had given the command, he would have just pulled the trigger.

I marched alongside the other women, watching the Taliban. They all looked like fierce animals who could attack us at any point. And then, as we walked, the Taliban started beating us. About thirty women were hit, but finally we managed to escape. A few of the Taliban carried on talking to each other and then they looked towards us and started laughing.

16:25

Shekiba

They attacked some journalists during the protest in Kabul. We tried to stand up for them but we didn't manage to protect them. The Taliban were constantly trying to keep us quiet; every few minutes we could see cars full of them arriving at the scene. I was scared and anxious because I felt the threat from the Taliban was increasing. Their special forces also arrived and started blocking our way. A few of us managed to get into the street. As I escaped, I looked behind me. One of the Taliban fighters

was running after the girls who'd crossed to the other side of the road. I wanted to cry. The day seemed so dark and scary. Even before I joined the protest, I feared the Taliban. Now I know how my fellow protestors felt – now I can feel all their pain and stress. But it's my life, and my choice, and I'm proud that I made the decision to protest. It's been an incredible experience. It's given me strength and I feel braver than ever before. Now I know that I can stand up for myself and my rights.

16:30

Fatima

I'm very proud of you, dear Shekiba. I hope you're OK!

16:32

Shekiba

Thank you, my dear. I'm fine.

16:37

Fatima

I hope everything gets back to normal.

19:51

Amina

I hope so too, but at the moment all my hopes and dreams are broken.

19:52

Mariam

Today I woke up more determined than ever; I decided to wear a pink headscarf as a contrast to the black colours I wear daily. I didn't realize how hard it is to win against the darkness of war. We have to pay a considerable price at every step. When the office car was driving from Karta-e-Mamorin towards Bagh-e-Bala, the Taliban stopped us at a checkpoint. The Talib fighter had long and dirty hair. He asked the driver to open the

windows and asked him, 'Where are you going?' The driver told him, 'We're all going to the office.' Then the Talib pointed at me and said, 'Who is she?' I was so scared. My heart started racing. My whole body was shaking. The driver was scared too. He said, 'She is our colleague.' The Talib replied in a rude tone, 'Tell her to wear appropriate clothes.' The driver wanted to get away, so he said, 'OK. I will tell her.' When the car moved away, my feelings changed just like the direction of the wind. I was not fearful anymore. I was angry. I felt humiliated. I asked myself, what should I wear? I'm wearing a long dress that covers me from head to toe. I'm all in black. Does he mean my pink scarf is not appropriate? I don't understand why everything is against women. What other humiliations should we expect in the future?

19:53

Samira

God is great, let's have faith. The whole system has collapsed, so it needs time to be re-established. Even during the presidential election, the situation was messy and felt chaotic. Now the whole government has collapsed, so this uncertainty is to be expected.

19:54

Mariam

Yes, but the wait is killing me.

19:55

Amina

I hope everything will be back to normal soon. Yesterday, my nephew saw gunfire as he drove through the streets in his car. The security situation is at its worst.

19:56

Fatima

I hope so. Due to COVID restrictions we haven't lived a normal life for the past five months, and now that the Taliban have come it's even more difficult to live normally.

19:57

AFGHANISTAN AND COVID

Afghanistan's healthcare system has come under pressure during many years of conflict. Before 2021, the Taliban attacked medical clinics and hospitals, forcing healthcare workers to flee. As a result, the government didn't have enough money to repair hospitals or deliver equipment to remote areas, so when the COVID pandemic hit, Afghanistan's medical facilities weren't equipped to care for people. There was a shortage of intensive care beds and oxygen for patients with breathing difficulties and the government couldn't afford to buy vaccines or to test people for COVID. By February 2022, only 10 per cent of Afghanistan's population had been vaccinated. In the capital Kabul, there was a period of lockdown, but the ongoing conflict meant it was hard to ask people with COVID to self-isolate. There were around 8,000 confirmed deaths from COVID, but the total was probably much higher as the Afghan government couldn't record all pandemic infection numbers.

Samira

We must remain positive. Negative thoughts will just stress us out even more at this difficult time.

20:09

Fatima

I will try my best.

20:09

12th September 2021

Nadia

After the protest my sister and I stayed behind. The other women were about fifty metres ahead of us, but we could not reach them. Haniya, my sister, was walking with her crutches. She was so tired. I told her last night that it might not be a good idea for her to join the protest, but she insisted on fighting for our freedom. The Taliban were passing by in their cars. I so wanted to shout out my slogan, but an elderly man said, 'Don't try to reach the protestors, you'll get lost in the crowd.' He was right. We couldn't reach the crowd of women, they were too far ahead.

I decided to throw my banner into the middle of the street so that both of us could go back home. We went via a mobile phone shop; it was full of men. We tried to pass through them, but some of them started making fun of us saying, 'Where are the other women? The ones that will give you your rights back?' The non-Taliban men were too scared to show support for us. We struggled through the male crowd.

Approaching the gate of Balkh, Haniya said, 'We should separate! You go home without me as you will be faster. Go straight home, and be careful – it's dangerous!'

I asked her, 'Can you manage to get home by yourself?'

She replied, 'Don't worry, I'll take public transport from here.' I pressed her hands tight in mine and told her to be careful. I

was scared. What if someone was following us? I was worried about her. She could not walk easily.

I took a local bus, sat close to another girl and tried to breathe deeply. I was wearing a mask so breathing was hard, and I could hear my heart beating. As soon as the bus started moving, I felt a bit calmer. After I got off the bus I walked into a quiet street and decided to change the coat I wore to the protest in case anyone could identify me. I just wanted to be safe. I walked very fast, put my scarf in my rucksack and tidied my hair. I was nearly home, but the whole way I was worried about Haniyeh. I didn't have my mobile on me to call her. When I got home, I found out she was fine and I could relax.

22:32

16th September 2021

Shekiba

Ladies, do you know that the Taliban are searching every house for the girls who protested? What should we do with our documents? I'm so worried and afraid. Someone told me, 'If you live in these districts (1, 2, 8, 7 and 5), you should try to move. Scan all your documents and send them to your family and friends via email so that there's a safe copy.'

When I hear all your anxious voices, I feel as if a thick smoke is rising, making it hard for me to breathe. I asked Nadia how things are in Mazar, but she didn't reply straight away. After a while she responded and said they were changing their route, and had stopped using the internet, in case they were traced. After this message, the group went silent and I prayed for each of the women who raised their voices against cruelty and injustice.

21:02

THE DIFFERENT PROVINCES OF AFGHANISTAN

Afghanistan has thirty-four provinces. Each province is then split into different districts. Each province has a capital and a governor who is the most important government official in the province. Afghanistan's largest province is Helmand in the south (about 58,000 km²), followed by Herat in the west and Kandahar in the south. The provinces with the largest populations are Kabul (about 5.2 million), which includes the national capital, Nangarhar in the east, Balkh in the north and Herat.

WHY DID THE TALIBAN WANT TO CONFISCATE PEOPLE'S PASSPORTS AND OTHER ID?

Afghans need a passport or ID documents to apply for a visa to travel abroad. Since the Taliban took over in 2021, passports from activists have been confiscated by the Taliban in order to prevent these protestors from travelling and reporting human rights abuses to other countries. This has made daily life in Afghanistan difficult as ID documents are often necessary to travel to certain parts of the country.

30th September 2021

> ## Samira
>
> Unfortunately, most of the women and girls who stood up against the Taliban were beaten, and some were arrested. Those women were just demanding justice and they were there to stand up for their basic human rights.
>
> The whereabouts of four of the young women who came out to protest against the Taliban is uncertain. They have been arrested because they were demanding their fundamental rights of education, work and freedom. This is their slogan: 'These rights are lawful and to stop us protesting is a sin in any religion.' At first, I thought the Taliban were only arresting girls who were protesting outside on the streets, but now they're dragging them out of their houses too. I worry so much about all of them and think about them, and all of us … What will happen to us?
>
> 16:14

As the Taliban got to grips with their new government, they enforced more restrictions on women – teenage girls were banned from going to school, they prevented women from working at many government offices and they stopped women travelling long distances without a male companion.

People struggled through a harsh winter and became poorer. The UN called the situation one of the worst humanitarian crises going on in the world today. Afghans who could, continued to escape to a more hopeful future. Others, like Nadia, continued to protest. The women had to become more organized because the street protests were very quickly and violently stopped by the Taliban.

Nadia

The struggle has changed. When we went to the streets to support the teachers' protest, we faced horrible treatment. The Taliban confiscated Haniya's and Shekiba's mobile phones, we had a verbal clash with them and we made a conscious decision to change the way we carried out our protests.
We called all the girls to meet up in a park – Chihil-e-Seton Gardens – so we were all together in one place. We decided to pretend we were having a picnic, but really we were calling all the journalists, from both national and international media, to tell the world about our peaceful protest.

As the journalists arrived we chanted for our rights and freedom. We demanded not be eliminated from society. The garden was soon filled with cars full of Taliban fighters. We didn't know who had told them about our gathering, but for us it was a success. The Taliban didn't arrest anyone from our group and that felt like a win. It was an exciting and scary experience for me to be among all these incredibly brave women. It also made us determined to make plans for more protests in the coming days. 'Long live the brave and courageous women of Afghanistan'!

06:27

7ᵗʰ May 2022

Samira

The restrictions on women by the Taliban have made many people worried, if not terrified. We face many problems in our country, but the only thing that the Taliban focus on is how to discourage, dishonour and insult women. It seems this is their main task. For me, just trying to imagine how the Taliban think is scary. Those of us who are still in Afghanistan cannot take the risk of protesting again. The consequences of going out could be grave, and those of you still going out are so brave and determined.

Today, I covered my eyes twice – once with my headscarf and then with my glasses on top – and I went to school to teach. Covering your face is bizarre for people who are not used to it. For those who are used to it, it's OK, but for my colleagues and me, this is very difficult. As soon as I entered the school, a question flashed through my mind: will the school be the same? But when I looked, everything seemed the same as before. I greeted all the school staff and chatted a bit with the other teachers. I found that the way the school looked hadn't changed, the equipment was the same, the chairs and desks were the same. But I soon realized that the whole system was different, and the school's curriculum was totally messed up. The Taliban had decided to change the girls' classes and move them to another school. All our students were boys now. I was so disappointed. Now the Taliban had changed all our timetables to segregate boys and girls, I had no choice but to leave the course and focus on my other job at the government school. It means I will lose money and I will

face financial problems. I have a strong belief that God knows best and he will find me a way, but I can't help being worried. We are a family of ten people, and I am the only breadwinner.

When we came out of the school, the Taliban vehicles drove past at high speed, and we felt scared. Every time the Taliban passes by we pray to God that everything will be alright. Hopefully, nothing terrible will happen to any of us.

16:50

9th May 2022

Amina

The Taliban has fought for many years against us women, but I never expected some of the men I know to turn against me, just because of my gender. This situation and these new restrictions give indirect power to all the men of our country, including our relatives. Hiding our physical shapes under a burqa is just one small part of it; the main aim of the Taliban is to cover our thoughts and ideology, our freedom of speech, our right to protest and our right to education. They want to put us in a box.

06:31

12th May 2022

Sola

Please don't stress about all this. Please don't let the Taliban's restrictions bring you down. Cover yourselves, wear glasses and protect us all against them and their ruling. Dear friends, what will become of us if we don't stand up for ourselves now?

15:31

Change:
Nothing Feels the Same Anymore

Soon after retaking Kabul, the Taliban put their own government in place and the writers shared with each other how they felt about these sudden changes to their everyday lives.

20th August 2021

Samira

My Kabul, the ruined city of my hope, the scorched earth of my dreams. I cannot see your green valleys, the rivers and your mountains anymore. I cannot see the white pigeons on the blue mosques. I cannot sit under the peach trees and speak with the

Buddhas of Bamyan anymore. I can only dream of the day that I throw away my burqa and walk tall in the streets of Kabul styling my hair with my hands, then I buy some street food and think I need one more bolani for someone else too. The other portion is for my beloved, who left a red rose on my desk at work. My dreams, which were carried on the wind like dandelion seeds, have been blown away once more. My dreams… My dreams…

12:42

25th August 2021

Samira

Change is a challenge. Girls like me find it difficult to accept another way of living; the Taliban do not want our society to progress, and I do not want to go backwards. Just like a burqa cannot cover the identity of a girl, the Taliban cannot stop this country having an inclusive government. I hope all these complications will be solved soon.

17:46

Amina

For more than forty years we have lived in a vicious circle in this country. Every time a new government is put on display to the world, it introduces tailor-made laws. Then people are stuck with them, like newly trained horses. No sooner have people got used to the new rules imposed on them than the pages turn again, and fresh new rules are introduced. Every human being across the land is tired of this circle. We don't know where we

are; we're tired and confused. We don't have a government; we don't have the right to go to work and we don't have the right to wear what we want. It's so painful.

18:02

Fatima

We are condemned to cruelty and brutality.

18:07

18ᵗʰ September 2021

Samira

One of my friends told me that her husband has been behaving differently since the Taliban took over. She complains that he doesn't listen to her now. Before, they used to discuss many matters and make joint decisions about life. But now he tells her that women's voices don't matter. She said, 'He told me to keep my mouth shut, to go and take care of the kitchen and cooking.' She also told me that her husband was speaking to his friend on the phone and they congratulated each other that women's rights were finally over. I don't think these men are to blame. When the authorities act against you, it can bring out unexpected sides in people you know.

I just opened my Facebook. I saw a clip from a TV programme where a mullah of the new government was saying, 'Women cannot go out of the house without a male companion and single women should get married.'

15:23

Fatima

In Afghanistan, if you are a woman and you wear the full hijab, you are considered a good woman – you are seen to be modest and have self-respect. Your hijab also depicts your innocence and shows that you are a good religious person. When a woman is covered from head to toe she has all the positive points of being a respected woman, but a woman who wears jeans is considered loose and deserves to be punished. For example, when I took a photo with my friend on the street, a middle-aged lady passed by and said, 'You're shameless! Go and take photos at home. The Taliban are here, aren't you scared? I hope they teach you some manners.' I wanted to respond, but I saw a motorbike coming towards us waving the flag of the Taliban and with a man holding guns. My friend and I hurried home, scared. I'm sure if we'd stayed the lady would have reported us to the Taliban and we would have been in trouble as my friend was wearing jeans.

17:53

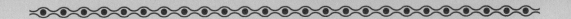
Nadia

Most of the alleys in the city are dirty and dusty. My shoes and trousers get dusty when I go out in the summer. Winter is coming and it's harder; sometimes I sink up to my knees in the mud and I get stuck. I walk the same path as thousands of other people. Each step I take, the dust from the alleys settles on my trousers, but I continue walking because I don't care how dusty I get, because I know cleanliness doesn't matter anymore; having a style is no longer important. In fact, the dustier you are, the more natural you look. You fit into society better. You're more easily acceptable to the Taliban.

These thoughts were in my head as I was walking today, until I reached the roundabout and I saw a big crowd of people. I went to see what the commotion was about. The Taliban had stopped a girl and they were shouting at her – all the people around her, mostly men, were staring. The girl was very scared. I asked one of the bystanders, 'What's going on?' He said, 'The Taliban didn't like that girl's appearance so they stopped her.' I asked if it was because some of her hair was showing. He replied, 'No, she's wearing jeans and has rolled them up. She's wearing headphones and came out of her house looking too stylish.' I just shook my head and walked away. I thought: in order to be accepted as women in this society we must dress the way the Taliban expect us to; we have to forget about what clothes we like and what we want to choose.

13:56

WHY DO THE WOMEN TALK ABOUT GOING BACKWARDS?

In 2001, after the US invaded Afghanistan and helped overthrow the Taliban, the doors of progress opened — Afghan women and girls now officially had the right to basic freedom. All girls were allowed to return to school and universities were full of young women. Afghan women participated in the country's politics and legal system — they were elected to parliament, were active in ministries and even stood for presidential elections. Women regained the freedom they'd lost during Taliban supremacy. But, when the Taliban returned to power in 2021, every aspect of women's lives changed again. Many women were banned from working in government offices and girls were not allowed to attend secondary school. This is why many Afghan women talk of going backwards.

It also refers to Afghanistan's long history of governments being overthrown through violent coups, rather than changing through democratic elections:

- In 1973, Mohammed Daoud Khan overthrew the king to become president.
- In April 1978, Daoud Khan was assassinated and Nur Muhammed Taraki took over, only to be overthrown in September 1978.

- Hafizullah Amin then became president, but he was killed when the Soviet Union invaded in 1979.
- Over the next seventeen years, Afghanistan had seven more presidents before the Taliban took over in 1996. Most of the presidents were overthrown, killed or forced to flee. People are afraid that Afghanistan will revert to yet more violence and uncertainty.

8th October 2021

Fatima

I've seen people desperately selling their belongings on Facebook. It's happening in Herat, Kabul and Mazar. You can see that some of the things are brand new. Afghan women have a habit of saving their best belongings and often only bring them out for special guests. Now they're selling these precious items. In the market, I saw a mattress which I'm sure belonged to a newlywed couple because of its particular style and size. When I see my home and I look around at all my things I feel like crying. I think back and remember that I bought every piece with so much hope and love. I feel terrible seeing people who have just started in life now having to sell everything to survive. I wish this was just a bad dream. There's really no point staying in the country now.

11:29

Samira

As I walked towards my home in Kabul, I passed Pul-e-Surkh roundabout. A few days ago, this was a place where all the educated people of Kabul came to buy books. But now it's completely different. It's too upsetting: I saw a little girl of five or six years old, begging for help. As I was getting on the bus I saw the girl had a younger sibling with her who didn't even have proper clothes on. The child was about two years old. Poverty is everywhere now the Taliban are here.

19:42

WHAT IS A HUMANITARIAN CRISIS?

A humanitarian crisis occurs when an event or series of events threatens the health, safety or well-being of a large group of people. It might be a war, or a natural disaster, such as an earthquake, flood or drought. In Afghanistan, years of conflict means many hospitals have stopped working and large numbers of refugees need to be housed. Many people lost their jobs and struggled to find enough food. If a poor country suffers a humanitarian crisis, it may need assistance from other countries to help look after casualties, house refugees or rebuild the places that have been destroyed. In Afghanistan, the main central bank funds were frozen by the US, so humanitarian crises worsened.

12ᵗʰ October 2021

Amina

The other day I went to the bank to get some money out. I only had 500 Afghani (about five pounds sterling) in my purse. The bank was full of people, on both floors. One bank employee told me, 'There's no money here.' The Taliban were threatening people with guns. Men and women were shouting and demanding to take out all their funds. Some were even crying and pleading for their money. I spent three hours there, but returned home empty-handed. I'm so afraid that everyone will soon lose hope.

I look outside the window and it's snowing heavily. It looks like about 20 cm of snow has settled. If this was a few years ago, I would have been jumping with joy because I love the snow. But I don't feel that joy today. I'm losing the confidence I've been trying to build all these years. I have no motivation to do anything. My mind keeps asking questions: When will everything be OK again? Why are we in this situation? How long will these regimes use the name of women and their rights as political tools? I have no answer.

13:12

Shekiba

I work in the media and I make radio programmes. Since the collapse of the republic, our work has stopped, though I keep in touch with my work colleagues through a WhatsApp chat group. We hear about the situation in our country from each other, we communicate about security matters and sometimes colleagues share advice and suggestions. We also find out who's been evacuated.

Yesterday I picked up my smartphone. As I turned it on, I saw a text from my manager saying the office would be opening on Sunday. We were invited to start work at 8 a.m. He also wrote that the women would need to sit in the back of the car, and that they would be working separately from the men in the office. The manager said he hoped that we'd all accept these changes. So I went into the office after a month away. Many of us women were glad to come back into work; with COVID we were fed up with staying at home. There was a printer on one side of our room. About every half an hour a male colleague would come in to print something. The last one to come was Farid. He had to knock on the door and check there weren't any woman near the printer so that he could come in. He was so nervous that he nearly tripped over as he entered our room. Everything's changed.

19:20

18th November 2021

Nadia

I wanted to get into one of the public transport cars, but the driver wouldn't allow me to sit in the front seat. When I asked why, he said, 'If you want to sit here then you have to pay for two people.' I asked him, 'Why should I pay for a second person?' At that moment another passenger said to the driver, 'Hurry up, let's go. We'll be late. If she wants to pay, she can stay. Otherwise, she needs to leave.' He added: 'Those times when we had to listen to women have passed.' Here in Afghanistan, people still think that when we talk about the rights of women it's Western propaganda; they think the West encourages women to go against men.

15:23

HOW DID PEOPLE STAY IN TOUCH AFTER THE TALIBAN TOOK OVER?

When the Taliban took over, it wasn't safe for many people to move and talk freely outside of their homes, so people used other means of communication, such as online messaging platforms, including WhatsApp. This made it harder for the Taliban to track the messages that people sent to organize protests. Some people used social media, such as Facebook or Twitter, when they wanted their messages to be seen by many people around the world. The Taliban also used social media to accuse protesters of spreading 'Western propaganda' (this is when someone spreads biased information to support their beliefs) when protesters posted information criticizing the Taliban government.

15th February 2022

Shekiba

Yesterday was Friday. After my prayers, I put my (prayer) beads made from olive stones into my pocket and went outside. I wanted to spend around half an hour in the park, but when I reached it the gate was closed. I was surprised because there were people inside. A vendor was selling corn at the gate. He shouted, 'Mother, the gate is closed.' I looked at him and smiled to thank him but went ahead anyway, as the park has another entrance on the north side. When I reached that gate a young boy called to me, 'Mother, what do you want?' I was surprised. He warned me not to go into the park. I asked him why. 'Don't you see there are no women in the park?' When I looked in, I got goosebumps. I couldn't see a single girl or a lady in there – it was full of men. The young boy laughed at me and said, 'There are specific days for ladies. Look at the timetable on the wall, can't you read it?' I didn't answer him. I looked at the timetable. It said: Sunday, Tuesday and Wednesday for ladies and the rest of the time for males only. Please follow the rules. Women and men aren't allowed to be at the park simultaneously. Two Talibs passed by with their guns and told me to leave immediately.

11:46

6ᵗʰ May 2022

Amina

When I went to the park, I saw that they had split it down the middle with a curtain to make separate spaces for men and women. There were no crowds like before, everything was different, and all the rides in the park were cheaper. I didn't use any of them, I just walked barefoot on the grass, but due to the segregation of the areas the walking distance was limited. I felt there was no fresh air anymore and I felt constrained in my designated female space. By the time it was 8 p.m., compared to before, the park was empty. The area seemed like a ghost city. My nephew said, 'It is not a ghost. It is the Taliban.'

11:13

THE TALIBAN'S DIFFERENT RESS FOR MEN AND WOMEN

The Taliban version of Sharia law affects men and women but it particularly affects women's freedom of choice. Women have been told to appear in public in hijab, and they can only travel long distances with a male relative. Girls are only permitted to attend primary school. Most women who had previously worked for the government were ejected and their jobs were given to men.

Men, however, are allowed to travel freely and work in any job. Boys of all ages can go to school and even go on to university. Under the first Taliban government, the rules were even stricter — women couldn't even travel on the same buses as men.

AFGHANISTAN'S PATRIARCHAL SOCIETY

For most of its history, Afghanistan was divided into areas controlled by tribes made up of different ethnic groups.

The various tribes have the authority that usually lies with the government. Each village has elders, always men, whose decisions must be obeyed, while women have very little say. Arguments between tribes are traditionally decided by a jirga or a meeting of the elders from each tribe. Throughout the history of the country, men have made key decisions inside and outside the home. Despite the risk, there have always been Afghan women who have been outspoken about society being so male dominated.

Since the Taliban took over in 2021, some Afghan men have shown support for women and women's rights in many different ways. For example, some male university lecturers have resigned from their jobs in protest at the Taliban's decision to ban all women from Higher Education.

Amina's Story

I'm currently not allowed to go to work in my office, so I've decided to go on a short trip. My late mother was born in Wardak province in a village called Jaghato. Now I'm a grandma, but because of war and insecurity in my country I still haven't seen that village. My uncle still lives there and he sometimes visits us in Kabul.

Recently, my son was excited because his uncle had called and asked him to accompany him to a party. He asked if he could go. I said it was fine, so he went. He was away for two days, and when he came back he told me he'd travelled to Ghazni province, which is close to Wardak. This made me really worried because Ghazni has been a battleground for the past few years, full of explosions and fighting, and most of the landscape has been destroyed. I've heard that the land is like a graveyard. But my son told me it's safe now, there's nothing to worry about, but I found this impossible to accept and I was concerned that he could have been in trouble. What if he'd said something against the new government? I was thankful when he returned, and I asked him about the journey and his trip to Ghazni. He said it was safe, and if I would like to visit my mum's village he would come along.

I called my uncle – he's been unwell, so I thought it would be good to go and see him. I took my wallet, counted my money and went to the market to buy some gifts. Then I packed my belongings for the trip.

The next day I woke up at 5 a.m., took my stuff from the wardrobe and got ready to go. I was still feeling very anxious. I took my chadari out. I'd bought it twenty-five years ago, when the previous Taliban government made them compulsory for women. Whenever I used to tidy my wardrobe, I would look at the chadari and think about how

expensive it had been. I hadn't worn it for over twenty years. Sometimes I would take it out of the wardrobe to throw it away – once I even left it outside my door, but no one touched it, so the next day I decided to take it back. I've often wanted to throw it away, but something would stop me, and I would think, what if I need it at some point?

Today I wore that chadari again to go to the village with my son. We took a taxi; the roads weren't crowded like they were before. The taxi driver was a young man of twenty-five years old. He said: 'Before, there used to be a lot of tanks and military vehicles on the way, and we were searched, which took a lot of time. The journey to Ghazni was six hours. Now the roads are empty and it's only three hours.'

I saw a few lorries ahead of our car: some families were moving home. A lady with her child was sitting in the back of one of the lorries. I could see the mother holding her kid tight to her chest. They were internally displaced families.

My son was sitting in the front seat and the driver was chatting to him. He said, 'The Taliban don't like women sitting in the front seat with a male driver.' I knew this from how they ruled last time. I was looking out of the car window: I couldn't see the National Army anymore, the soldiers who defended this land and paid the price with their blood. Looking out, I also saw little girls passing in school uniforms with their blue UNAMA bags. Far away from the city this view gave me hope.

When we finally arrived in Wardak province, I got out of the car. It was a two-and-a-half-hour walk to my uncle's house. My cousin called me and said he'd be waiting for us near a green villa. It's in a village that no government has been able to fully control. People there produce all their own food, from flour to milk and vegetables. The men of the family usually travel to the city a few times a year to shop for other needs like soap.

As soon as I reached the village, my cousins and my uncle's grandchildren came to the front of the villa to welcome us. The silence of the village was broken by the sound of cows and children playing outside.

It was fascinating. The atmosphere was full of joy. Smoke from tandoors (clay ovens) was coming out of the houses. We had lunch, and as we chatted I asked my uncle if someone might hurt them because I'd come from Kabul to visit. He said, 'No, there hasn't been anything like that happening.' He added, 'I spent forty-two years in the war and I've never seen or felt so much peace around. I'm glad the foreign invasion is over. I'm happy that the bombs have stopped.' My uncle's wife said, 'I hope those times never come back; the new government has brought peace.'

There was a photo on the wall with flowers around it. My uncle's wife said, 'That's my son. He was in prison for five years and then released. He died in an American drone strike.' I said, 'Afghanistan is the graveyard of young men – police officers, soldiers, engineers. It's also the graveyard of children and women.'

My son and I spent two days without TV, radio, internet and the loud noise of the city.

MOVING AROUND THE COUNTRY

In 2021, as the Taliban tried to take control of certain provinces, there was fighting across the whole of Afghanistan. Many people didn't travel for fear of being caught in the conflict. Government soldiers set up roadblocks to stop and search vehicles, hopeful of finding people who were working with the Taliban. In Taliban-controlled areas, soldiers stopped cars and buses in their hunt for government sympathizers.

Once the Taliban took full control of the country, there was no more fighting between the Taliban and the Afghan army in the provinces, and the country as a whole became relatively safer. It was possible for Afghans to travel by car at any time of day. However, the Taliban also placed restrictions on women travelling alone and punished anyone seen to be breaking these rules.

VILLAGE VERSUS URBAN LIFE IN AFGHANISTAN

Only about a quarter of Afghans live in towns or cities. The rest live in villages and experience much greater poverty as there aren't many jobs outside of farming. Also, away from towns and cities, people's views tend to be more conservative, with the village elders making most decisions. When foreign money or aid is given to Afghanistan, people in villages don't receive very much of it, which is why there is some distrust in the government in Kabul. Many villagers believe that no matter who is in power or the head of government, positive change is unlikely. They say that the Taliban victory and the withdrawal of the US and allied troops has at least brought peace back to the country.

28th November 2021

Nadia

Here in the city, the house above ours has just been rented after a long time. The family has two daughters. One is ten years old and the other is seven. I often listen to their words and laughter. They are as talkative and happy as sparrows. They usually play together in the afternoons and take on different roles. I spy on them through the curtains. Today, one appeared as a schoolgirl and the other as a Taliban. The schoolgirl was screaming and begging not to be hit. But the girl who played the Talib continued to hit her sister, saying,

'Your shirt is too short! Why did you come to school without a scarf?' When I saw that scene, I saw how this horror has spread into all parts of our lives and how it eats away our spirits like termites. Even children are no exception.

15:23

Samira

That's awful! How could the presence of the Taliban become a children's game so quickly? I feel like this country is a cage. Some are satisfied with a captive life, but the free birds are the ones who suffer.

15:29

Fatima

'Life will carry on,' said a young girl sitting close to me on the public bus. I wanted to respond and say, lucky you, you are hopeful and have a vision. To me everything feels blunt. It's been more than a month since I put on any make-up. I'm losing hope day by day. Even sitting by the window in the car and looking outside isn't pleasant anymore.

15:35

Mariam

My daughter has also noticed the situation. When I go out, she distances herself from me, and she's often silent. The minibus is often silent, unlike before. The driver doesn't sing and the girls aren't dressed in colourful clothes; those of university age just put their heads down, and their laughter no longer fills the air. When will we hear the music of laughter again?

15:55

Flee:
Time to Go

Afghans have been fleeing their country since 1979 to escape persecution and human rights abuses. While many may have returned, there are 2.3 million Afghans registered as refugees, mostly in neighbouring Pakistan and Iran. A further 180,000 Afghans have sought asylum since the beginning of 2021. After the Taliban took over for a second time, tens of thousands of Afghans who were working with Western countries were evacuated. Sola was working for a German organization who made it possible for her to reach Germany. Mariam travelled to Sweden via unofficial channels, while Nadia and Amina searched desperately for a way out of the country.

26th August 2021

Sola

Every day our house is full of friends and relatives who come to visit. They're all stressed out and scared. Each of them is begging me to help. They say, 'You're educated. You can find a route to take us out of here.' These words make me even more stressed. I can't tell them I can't do anything because I know they'll feel as hopeless as me. I try my best to help in any way I can. I tell them to bring me their ID and I'll try to register them, but I can't do anything more. I don't want to disappoint them. I remembered something from a TV show, where the main character says, 'You either play or they will play with you.' The same is true for us: life has been playing with us for so many years.

16:05

20th October 2021

Samira

Today the passport department started operating again. A crowd of more than three hundred people came to get passports. Like me, most people queued to have their photo taken. We've been waiting for hours. They're not allowing people in, so we just have to wait.

07:36

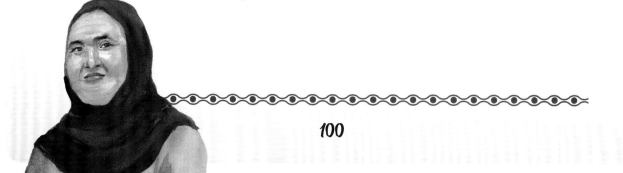

Nadia

I waited for three hours in front of the passport office of Balkh province hoping that I could get the forms for a passport application. I was with my sister – we waited and waited but were just disappointed. Some people came to extend the date of their passport, others came to apply for a new one. Today I saw that there will be another round of applications. They're issuing limited visas for students and people who need to travel for medical treatment. We know there are many wealthy people who have contacts at the passport office, and they'll get out first. We're the victims. We don't have any contacts. My sister feels hopeless and is terrified of the current situation. I hope I can get her out of the country soon.

09:14

Sola

I was contacted by my German employers and told to gather all my travel documents. Maybe I will go next week, and I will leave my country forever. I try to stay happy, but it's hard. My family, parents, siblings and friends will all stay behind under the grey sky with all these scary men on the streets. They'll have to continue to breathe here and live here. I'm worried about how my mum will handle this separation. All her children are going away from her one after another at a time when she needs them the most. When I think about my father, this man who is so patient and brave, my heart breaks. I'm scared that my parents will grow old and weak, and I won't see them again. I can't stop my tears.

10:19

22nd October 2021

Mariam

Hello, girls. I hope wherever you are, you're OK. After a very long journey I've finally arrived in Sweden. I hope all of you get somewhere safe soon.

20:57

Fatima

Thank God you reached there safely.

21:43

23rd October 2021

Nadia

Dear Mariam, thanks for the good news. I'm glad you've arrived OK. I wish you all the best.

16:10

Mariam

May God bless you all.

16:20

Samira

All the best, my dear. I hope one day none of us have to leave our home and country.

17:10

HOW AFGHAN MIGRANTS TRAVELLED TO OTHER COUNTRIES

Without the correct travel visas and other official documents, citizens intent on fleeing often have no other choice than to turn to people-smugglers. In return for large sums of money, a people-smuggler helps refugees without visas or paperwork cross a country's borders, and this has continued since the Taliban took over in 2021. Travelling at night in small groups, the smugglers drive refugees to the border and cross with them on foot. Some people-smugglers in Afghanistan have escorted refugees to Iran. From Iran, some are transported to Iran's border with Turkey. In Turkey, some travel to the Aegean Sea to take overcrowded boats to the Greek islands or mainland. Some refugees also cross Turkey's land border into Bulgaria or Greece. Many refugees continue to cross different borders in secret until they reach a country where they feel safe enough to claim asylum, such as Germany or Sweden.

Sola

I told my father that I may have a flight next week. He smiled and seemed happy for me. I felt that he was faking his happiness so I wouldn't get upset. I said to him, 'It's not too late. If you want me to stay, I'll stay.' He replied, 'No, you have to leave, there is nothing for you here anymore. Go and follow your dreams. If destiny brings us together, we'll see each other again; if not, I leave it to God to protect you.' His words break my heart. I feel like I'm losing him.

09:11

Amina

We must try to keep hope, dear Sola. Dear Mariam, I'm glad you've arrived safely and wish you a happy life there.

09:26

Mariam

Thank you all. I wish you all the best. I'm glad I'm safe, but my heart still wants peace and prosperity for everyone. It wants the same peace the people have here in their home country. They walk freely and go wherever they want. They climb mountains. I want to climb our own mountains and scream that I want a free, peaceful country, without the cruelty of the Taliban. I want a land full of kind humans who think positively.

10:11

25th October 2021

Shekiba
Mariam, I miss you. I'm still in Kabul. I hope you don't forget us, my dear.

06:31

Mariam
Hello, dear Shekiba. I miss you too and your kids! I had no other option. I hope you also manage to leave soon for a safer country.

17:29

28th October 2021

Shekiba
I'm thinking about renting out my house in order to travel and move from here. I'm OK with this, because I'm not emotionally attached to my house, but no one should feel pushed out of their home and country. No one should be forced or told to go away. If only I was in better health.

14:30

THE RISKS PEOPLE TOOK IN ORDER TO LEAVE AFGHANISTAN

Some Afghan refugees walked across high mountain ranges to reach the border of Pakistan, where they then had to climb over high barbed-wire fences. Others waded and swam across deep rivers to traverse the border into Tajikistan. To cross into Iran, refugees had to travel across the Dasht-e-Margo, or Desert of Death, which is incredibly hot. Once in Iran, the border with Turkey was blocked by ditches and a three-metre-high wall. Some made their way to Turkey in lorries that didn't have enough air, resulting in death by suffocation. Refugees who reached west Turkey often travelled to Greece in small boats that weren't seaworthy — many drowned.

3rd November 2021

Sola

Dear friends, I have a flight tomorrow. This whole week I have tried to act happy, so my parents think that I'm pleased I can finally leave Afghanistan and reach safety. I don't want to add to their worries. I say to myself, I must suffer this pain alone. I must keep this heavy burden away from my family. I pack my luggage and close it with sadness. I still joke with my parents and try to break the silence in the house. My mother says she wants to go to bed early because she has a lot to do, but I know she goes and cries in her room. I don't say anything.

09:40

Fatima

Thank God you're leaving too. I've reached Tajikistan.

13:44

Mariam

Have a good journey, dear Sola.

16:37

Sola

Thank you, dear Mariam and Fatima. I hope you're safe and happy.

17:09

4ᵗʰ November 2021

Fatima

My anxiety is increasing day by day. Leaving my family behind felt like the worst decision of my life. When I wake up in the mornings here, I feel scared that the internet might be cut off in Afghanistan and I might not hear from my family. But when I see that my family members have texted me, I feel much better. I've been feeling anxious ever since the day when I was speaking to my mum and she was suddenly cut off and I couldn't contact her for several hours. After a long wait I received a message from my sister telling me they're OK – the electricity had gone down. It was a very frightening few hours and it left me feeling traumatized.

17:50

Sola

When the aeroplane took off, it occurred to me that it might be the last time I would see my country. I looked at Afghanistan's dry and angry land from above and I felt fire in my heart. As the aeroplane was going up, my emotions melted like ice inside me and vanished. Many people cried during the flight, why couldn't I?

12:06

6th November 2021

Sola

It's 6 November. I was born on this day, and it's my first proper day in Germany. I almost feel like I've been born again and I'm starting a new life. I wished myself a happy birthday and hoped for the

best of luck in the new life I'm facing on my own. I looked at my phone. My mother had sent me a picture of a birthday cake. I was happy, but sad at the same time. I wanted to be reunited with my family and not be a refugee. My birthday wish was a silent one – that no one else ever becomes a refugee like me.

13:04

20th November 2021

Amina

No matter where I go, I hit a brick wall. Will I get a passport or not? The passport office is closed, I want to get my ID card, but the registrar's office is closed until further notice. I want to go to register my marriage certificate but it's the same story. In reality, all the doors are closed these days. Which era are we living in? Other countries seem to care about how they are seen by the rest of the world, but here it is the opposite: the Taliban want us to surrender unconditionally. It's suffocating when you feel like a prisoner in your homeland.

14:52

22nd November 2021

Sola

It's been three months since the Taliban took over. As I write this, I'm on the road in Germany. I don't know where they're taking us, but I can read from the road signs that we're travelling towards Düsseldorf. We arrived in this country after thirteen hours of travelling. My legs are aching, and my ears

are tired from the loud crying of a child who was sitting next to me on the plane. Although I made it out of the cursed land, I'm not happy. Others on the same flight were talking about life in Germany and their future. I had no butterflies in my stomach; I was cold and emotionless.

    As I write, many of my colleagues on the bus are sleeping, and the only sound I can hear is rain, but I can't sleep.

07:39

24th November 2021

Mariam

I reassure myself by saying that it's a bad dream. I keep telling myself: 'You're in your own home right now. You're sleeping in your warm bed. There's no hardship.' But I know this is not reality. I can't sleep. I'm wide awake, living through the present situation. I'm without a homeland and my home. The clothes I'm wearing are from the local charity. Everyone here in Sweden welcomes the Afghan refugees, but I feel dizzy and I can't smile. I'm broken, my self-esteem is hurt, I feel hopeless. I wonder if we deserve all this. I'm a refugee and a homeless person, this is the reality that I have to accept.

23:42

27th November 2021

Sola

I'm trying to be happy in Germany. I went with other girls to shops and restaurants, but nothing attracted me; it was as if my

friends had brought a dead body with them. Every time I want to do something, I think about my family, and everything becomes bitter. The day of the flight I felt terrible. My mother's sad look and my father's shivering hands broke me. I don't know when we will see each other again. My siblings didn't say anything, but I felt what they were going through – happiness combined with pain and sorrow. That feeling can make you crazy.

11:32

28th November 2021

Fatima

I'm like a turtle carrying a heavy stone on its back. When I carry my backpack, I feel the weight on my whole body. I think immigrants and refugees are like birds: they travel from one

place to another all the time. When you're a refugee every little thing that you carry becomes heavy on your shoulders. You must learn to stop missing people who were around you – your loved ones, your friends, the ones with whom you cried and laughed. You miss your soil, the soil that you belong to. When you leave home, you feel restless, it feels like you're losing your identity. You can't sleep and you learn to accept humiliation and to remain silent. Yes, this is how you feel when you become a refugee. You are like those birds, or that turtle with a heavy load.

14:44

MIGRANTS, ASYLUM SEEKERS AND REFUGEES

- A **MIGRANT** is someone who leaves their own country to live or work in another country.
- An **ASYLUM SEEKER** is a person who asks for protection from another country because they are at risk of persecution in their home country.
- A **REFUGEE** is someone who cannot stay in their own country and is forced to leave. This may be because of war, or natural disasters like floods or drought, or because their government persecutes them for their religious, political beliefs or sexuality. There are about 26 million refugees worldwide.

Fatima

The sky was clear, and the sun was shining this morning. I started my day feeling positive; my heart was telling me that I would hear some good news. I wore my formal clothes. The weather was a bit cold, so I put on my warm coat. I left home feeling hopeful because I've heard that the United Nations (UN) office is helping journalists and young people from Afghanistan to gain asylum in countries like the US and Canada. These countries have said that Afghans at risk – and those like me, living in a third country – can apply for asylum. I live in Tajikistan now, so I set off to the UN office in the hope that I will find help.

13:33

WHAT IS A 'THIRD COUNTRY'?

According to international law, countries must accept refugees provided the refugees can prove they are at risk of persecution in their home country. The exception to this rule comes when a refugee has travelled through a 'safe' country – often called a 'third country' on their way to their final destination. The final destination has the right to send the refugee back to the 'third' country. There is plenty of debate about whether countries such as Turkey or Tajikistan should actually be regarded as 'safe' for refugees seeking sanctuary.

2nd January 2022

> **Mariam**
>
> When I close my eyes, I see my old self: the writer. I return to the time when I would grab my backpack and go out to report on the stories I had planned. I worked hard with love and passion. But when I open my eyes, I am not this person. I don't feel like a human. I don't want to accept what has happened to my country. I find it hard to see the future. I want all the changes to be unreal, so I close my eyes again.
>
> Since I'm here now, I don't want to forget who I am and where I come from. I will do my best to raise the voice of my people and be heard by everyone. I'm sure my voice will finally reach God. I'm longing for the day when my people will be free again.
>
> 11:59

4th January 2022

> **Fatima**
>
> I arrived at the UN office; I saw big luxury cars with the UNHCR logo on them parked there. I knocked on the door but there was no response. I waited, but still there was no response, so I pressed the doorbell. A man popped his head out of the small window and asked what I wanted. I said I'm Fatima, an Afghan journalist, and I want to talk to the people in charge. The man replied curtly, 'It doesn't matter who you are, all the staff are on leave due to COVID. And the director doesn't want to see you.' I asked if I could have a number or email to contact them. He responded, 'No!' and he shut the

window and left. I was very disappointed. I felt sad on my way back home; I kept thinking, what's the point of this office? It's a refugee agency, but they don't listen to refugees. We don't have any kind of support here. The sun didn't feel so shiny anymore. I started walking back home.

14:32

WHAT IS THE UN?

The United Nations (UN) was set up in 1945. It was established to create a peaceful bond between countries with the hope of preventing another large-scale conflict like the Second World War. There are 193 member states. Most governments across the world have signed the 1951 United Nations Refugee Convention, a document which sets out a refugee's rights, plus when countries must grant asylum. The UN makes sure that they fulfil the promises made in the convention.

A part of the UN called the United Nations High Commission for Refugees looks after the interests of refugees, particularly in the case of humanitarian emergencies. It might, for example, build and organize a camp for refugees.

Another part of the UN called the Security Council passes resolutions that condemn certain actions by countries and call for them to change, as with the Taliban's human rights violations.

Sola

Viersen is a charming city, with a pleasant nature, and pretty houses decorated with vases and flowers that add to its beauty. There are tall trees, and the footpaths are full of their red and yellow leaves. There are cycle routes on the side of the roads, and you have to say hi to everyone who passes by. On sunny days the city looks like a newlywed bride under the blue sky, easy on the eye. The dew on the leaves, the fresh air and the trees uplift the spirits of everyone here. I saw a small shop in a quiet corner near the river, where ducks were dancing in groups. The shop owner was a well-dressed and friendly old man. He could speak English. I asked for a coffee, and he gave me one with a smile.

Unconsciously I walked towards a tall hill, which reminded me of my childhood. I remembered a cartoon about the Alps in Europe. My childhood memories make me happy, and I wanted to walk towards the mountains and the forest. I thought about Lucien (a cartoon character), who forgot about his loneliness by making wooden tools in the wilderness. He was always happy when he returned home. When I was a child, I longed to experience the life of such a person. Big hills and forests, one-floored houses and big roads. When I saw the green fields in Germany, I remembered those images from my childhood. It was like a beautiful dream, and when I thought about it, I felt happy. I felt like Lucien, the son of a farmer. He had many hardships, and felt much fear and loneliness.

Despite these difficult times, I imagined my childhood once again and felt happy. But underneath, I kept asking myself, how are my friends coping under the Taliban regime back home?

16:04

no teenage
girls until
further notice

Education:
What Next?

In September 2021 the Taliban announced that while all boys were permitted to continue going to school, girls could only attend primary school. The Taliban's message around girls' education has been unclear from the moment the group took power. In August, a Taliban spokesperson said the new regime was 'committed to the rights of women' as long as they followed strict Islamic rules. In December, another official said that girls would not be allowed to attend secondary school until a new education policy was approved. More than a year later, that policy had still not been announced and millions of teenage girls remain deprived of an education. In some parts, even universities are shut for women.

The news of school closures was devastating for women and girls, particularly for teachers like Samira, and students like Nadia, who found it hard to keep up with all the changes happening around her.

Amina

Dear friends, the Taliban have announced that all boys can start going to school but they have stopped girls from attending secondary school. How can they do this? Girls are like glowing lights in the middle of a dark night. The Taliban have turned off the lights. I'm sure they won't allow women to go to university. I'm scared of the day when Afghanistan will go into complete darkness.

13:33

Nadia

Today's girls are not the ones from twenty years ago. The Taliban can never keep them away from education. If the Taliban deprive girls like this, they won't last even two years. A society that has woken up cannot go back to sleep so easily. The Taliban have said that they'll open schools for all girls gradually. They know if they don't do this, they'll be under international pressure.

15:07

Samira

I sat in the car and opened my Facebook; I read a post which said, 'Girls only up to year six can go back to school, and the rest will not be allowed.' The post said that it might be another year before teenage girls can come to school. The situation is so complicated that no one knows what will happen. The news is coming from every corner of the country.

10:23

Nadia

Ahhh, my heart is aching. I saw a video of a young girl on social media. She was crying because of the school closures. As I watched her, all my hopes started fading in front of my eyes. I try to stay positive. I just think: if one side of life is dark, the other side will be bright. I hope the schools are only delayed in opening and they will reopen soon. I hope this time the darkness of ignorance and oppression doesn't come back to Afghanistan. Girls are rebellious, strong and determined. They are so intelligent, but in this country they have to suffer so much. A storm of ignorance has hit Afghanistan. We should not allow it to blow out the lights of literacy in our country.

11:30

GIRLS' EDUCATION

During the first Taliban government's rule, women and girls weren't allowed an education. In 2021, the Taliban said that girls could continue to learn across all age groups, but when schools opened in September, the Taliban broke its promise and girls were not allowed to attend. Shortly after, the Taliban stated that girls could attend primary school only — no secondary school or university. The Taliban's approach to girl's education remains contradictory. They have changed the rules about education for older girls and women multiple times.

Shekiba

My nieces – Samina, eighteen years old, and Fahima, sixteen – both study at a private school in grade twelve. They only have one term left to complete their secondary education. When they heard this news, they both got angry and felt quite hopeless. I asked them round for tea and sat with them. When I looked at them, they started laughing and being cheeky. I asked what was happening. Samina said, we want to go to school tomorrow, please support us. I stared at them with surprise and asked: Aren't the schools closed? What if the Taliban sees you? How will you defend yourselves? They said, 'Don't worry. We only want to go to see our teachers; we've been planning this with our classmates.' I felt so proud of their determination.

18:20

Nadia

I felt heartbroken by today's announcement. We're getting closer to winter. In the past, at this time of the year I would be going to university, wearing my autumn make-up and clothes. I would walk there with my friends. We would discuss our upcoming exams and enjoy our freedom. But this year, the autumn is not the same; I'm stuck at home. I try to keep my courage going, but I don't see my friends anymore. I do embroidery all day long because I have to finish it by the end of the week. Our life has become all about how we can earn money to buy food. It's a strange feeling; just three months ago I was thinking about what university to choose for my master's degree.

19:09

WOMEN IN THE WORKPLACE

Since the Taliban took over in August 2021, many Afghan women who worked as journalists, as lawyers or for the government lost their jobs. In other offices, factories or headquarters, women aren't allowed to work alongside men. Instead, women must do the jobs that the Taliban think no man can do — for example, doctors and nurses that look after women only, administrators or secretaries in passport offices and at security checks, or in places that only have female customers.

19ᵗʰ September 2021

Shekiba

This morning, Fahima and Samina set off wearing hijabs. They looked just like any other women in public. They shouted goodbye as they passed my house, and I thought about how gorgeous they used to look in their school uniform every morning, with their dark green tops, black-checked skirts and black scarves.

They came to see me later in the day and were so happy that they had met their teachers and classmates even if they were not allowed to study.

14:09

10ᵗʰ October 2021

Amina

People are under pressure day by day. In the few months since the Taliban have been in power, everyday human rights have been violated, mainly affecting women. The government will continue to impose strict rules on us to cover their own flaws. The last law they imposed about hijabs is so useless it's hilarious. It states if a woman doesn't fulfil the hijab requirements, she will be given advice, and if she doesn't listen, they will punish her. In the third stage, they will imprison her. I understand from this newly imposed law that the Taliban will hire a Talib for each woman and follow her to see if she is fully covered or not, which is impossible. Is this how government works? This is the sad and bitter reality of Afghan women's painful and overwhelming life.

02:50

18th October 2021

Samira

A few days ago, I saw one of my former students, Reza, selling grapes from a trolley in town. I felt terrible for him. His father was a soldier. If the government hadn't collapsed and his father hadn't lost his job, he might have been at school now. When a teacher thinks about the future of her students, she imagines them as doctors, engineers or teachers. But I know the future for my students is very uncertain. When Reza said hi to me, he told me he wants to go to Iran as he can't earn enough here. I feel bad for the whole generation of tomorrow, the ones who lost their livelihoods and the ones who became refugees.

13:30

WHY WERE BOYS SENT TO WORK AFTER THE TALIBAN TOOK OVER?

When the Taliban took over, many families lost income as the women weren't allowed to work. To earn more money, families would make the decision to pull their sons out of school in order to find jobs. Although it has been illegal since 2007 for Afghans under the age of fourteen to seek employment, around 25 percent of children in the country work in bakeries, mines, carpet factories and more. As of 2023, more and more boys

work by collecting scrap metal or bottles that can be
reused, washing cars, pushing handcarts for vegetable
sellers or polishing the shoes of passers-by. The boys
only earn a few dollars a day, but this money is vital
for their families.

Amina

I woke up at midnight. I tried to go back to sleep but I
couldn't. I felt that even sleep had gone to take refuge
somewhere else. I got up, passed through the dark living
room and went into our little yard. The wind was strong, and
the leaves on the trees looked as if they were dancing. I sat in
a corner and gazed at the universe and the countless stars.
The sky was glorious, the moon was bright, and there was
a fresh breeze in the air. I looked up and said: 'God! Before
all the fleeing, before the capture of the cities, before people
abandoned their homes, my dream was just to live my life.'
Allah, I don't have anything to do with the president who ran
away. I don't want to be reminded of those dark days and
the chaos at the airport. I want to ask you for mercy. I felt my
prayers to God were tiny compared with the universe I was
looking at. I was speaking to my God, and I felt better.

00:25

Nadia

Women in my province (Balkh) stay at home mostly. They're kind of used to it as it's the norm – the effects of a long war. I don't think this situation will change any time soon. The girls and women of Afghanistan who live in the villages don't know the outside world. They work around the house all day without a break. Girls in many villages in my country don't make decisions, they wait for others to do it for them. Members of the family decide who they will marry. The girls call it destiny. It feels like there's a gap of a century between village and city life. We are going backwards now.

10:33

23rd March 2022

Samira

I opened my eyes and moved my blanket away as usual. I took out my mobile phone and went online, checking my messages. My colleague had left a message saying, 'Where are you girls?' Reading this made me smile. I replied, 'We're coming.' I stood up and got ready. I had missed my older students so much. I was so excited that I would be seeing all of them today. Many younger students were there, but I couldn't see the teenage girls anywhere. During break time, I went online and asked my school group why the girls weren't present. But then I saw a noticeboard which said, 'Teenage girls are not allowed until further notice!' I sighed loudly; it was the worst news I'd read so far. It made me really stressed, and I thought to myself, so this means all my beloved students are not coming to school.

During the last government, I didn't earn a good amount of money as a teacher, but now under the Taliban it's even worse. I remember looking for many good teaching jobs in the past, but because there was so much corruption, I wasn't successful. It was hard for people like me who didn't have money or contacts. I don't know what to do, and God knows what will happen. Every time the government changes, we suffer. Everywhere I look, I feel hopeless and sad.

11:02

23rd May 2022

Shekiba

On my way to work this morning I looked at all the ads on big boards for private schools in Kabul. I had hoped to see the roads busy just like before. They used to be full of construction workers and advertisements. In the past, this time of the year was very busy in Kabul. The whole city would be full of ads for new schools, courses, universities and teacher training courses. They were written in nice colours and made the city beautiful. Today I can't see any of those advertisements. There's no colour. We even had educational programmes on radio and TV stations every day. But now we don't have any. I'm very worried.

14:47

LIFE FOR GIRLS
IN AFGHAN VILLAGES

Before the Taliban took over Afghanistan in 2021, many girls in cities attended secondary school and university, but that was not the case in Afghan villages. In rural areas, girls sometimes stayed at home and got married. Some were married before they were sixteen years old, without ever having learned to read or write. They had little chance of becoming teachers, doctors or lawyers, and they were excluded from making any decisions that impacted their family or village. Without being able to read or write, they could not access the internet. As a result, it was hard for them to learn about the outside world or how their life could perhaps be different.

Samira

Last week, a Taliban official came to visit our school. There were many teachers out in the yard. He passed through the female teachers but only said hello to the male ones. I was told to be prepared for this: he doesn't greet women. But I insisted on meeting him. I thought, I'm also one of the teachers and we should meet. I said this out loud, and the Talib heard me. Someone from inside the office shouted, 'Have you ever seen me speaking to women? I never do, and now you're asking me

to talk to you face to face?' I went quiet and thought to myself that, in reality, the Taliban doesn't count women as human beings. But how can they progress in society if they won't rely on women and work with them? We may sink in ignorance.

15:31

25th May 2022

Amina

Yesterday, my granddaughter in the first grade went to school with a white headscarf – before the Taliban she didn't wear one. Unlike me, who is still not used to tightening my headscarf properly, she wore her scarf beautifully and very tidily. I said 'well done' to her for wearing her hijab so nicely. However, in my heart, I felt sorry for her. She's still a child, but she's started wearing a hijab out of fear of the Taliban. Why does she have to cover her head from the age of seven? I never saw her with this before. Here in Kabul, younger girls didn't use to cover their heads.

15:12

27ᵗʰ May 2022

Shekiba

My nieces insisted on going shopping and buying some school essentials. They've been doing this for years. We used to go shopping together at this time of the year to get new shoes, headscarves, socks, schoolbags, notebooks, pens, coloured pencils and pencil cases. Today there were only a few shops open. I asked a shopkeeper when the school uniforms would be out in the market. He asked if I wanted girls' or boys' uniforms. I said girls' – I want to buy a uniform for my nieces. He sighed and replied, 'Girls' time has passed. No one likes to make girls' school uniforms anymore.' We don't know if the Taliban will allow girls to go to school or not. My nieces pulled my hand and said we should leave. They didn't want to listen to him anymore. We went to another shop, and the shopkeeper said the same thing. We came home, and the girls were very sad. They were asking me, 'What will we do if the schools don't reopen?'

For now, there are no signs of schools and universities reopening for girls. I try to encourage my nieces to read books and get general information whenever possible. When I see them reading books at home it makes me so happy.

10:12

Conclusion:

WHAT HAPPENS NOW?

In 2023, no girls will graduate from government-run schools or go to university; poverty has increased, and only a limited number of women are working. The Taliban government is still not recognized internationally, and Islamic State (IS) has increased its attacks. However, the country is not at war, and for many Afghans like Shekiba, Amina, Samira and Nadia, day-to-day life is safer. Those who have fled Afghanistan and who now live in other countries like Sola, Mariam and Fatima, try to stay connected to their friends and family and hope to be able to return to their homeland one day.

ABOUT UNTOLD NARRATIVES CIC

Untold Narratives works to develop and amplify the work of writers marginalized by community or conflict. Its editors and translators work collaboratively with writers to develop their craft, connect them to one another and share their stories with readers worldwide.

The diary excerpts used in *Rising After the Fall* are drawn from a collective year-long diary created as part of Untold's Write Afghanistan project. They are written by: Zainab Akhlaqi, Marie Bamyani, Freshta Ghani, Naeema Ghani, Batool Haidari, Fatema Haidari, Elahe Hosseini, Masouma Kawsari, Fatema Key, Maryam Mahjoba, Atifa Mozzaffari, Maliha Naji, Anahita Gharib Nawaz, Parand, Sharifa Pasun, Fatima Saadat, Farangis Elyassi Saboor and Rana Zurmaty.

untold-narratives.org

ABOUT THE EDITORS

Lucy Hannah is the founder and director of Untold Narratives CIC. She is also a visiting research fellow at King's College, London, and a director of the Bocas Lit Fest in Trinidad and Tobago. She is the author of the children's book *Nancy Wake: World War Two Secret Agent 'The White Mouse'* (2006).

Zarghuna Kargar is an award-winning journalist for BBC World News, based in London. She produced and presented the BBC's *Afghan Woman's Hour* and is the author of *Dear Zari: The Secret Lives of Women in Afghanistan* (2012). She is one of the translators on Untold's Write Afghanistan project. She speaks Pashto, Farsi, English and Urdu.

EDITORS' ACKNOWLEDGEMENTS

On behalf of Untold Narratives we want to thank Dr Negeen Kargar, who translated the original Afghan diaries into English from Dari and Pashto. Thanks also to translators Khoshhal Taib and Dr Zubair Popalzai. The translation of this collective Afghan women's diary was made possible with support from the Bagri Foundation.

A special thank you to Parwana Fayyaz and Pashtana Durrani for their continued commitment to Untold's Write Afghanistan project. Also to Lillie Toon, for helping us to adapt the diary, and to Amy St Johnston at Aitken Alexander Associates, for her invaluable advice and support.

Thank you to Leah James, who believed in this book from the start, and to Elizabeth Scoggins, Jonny Marx, Richard Smith and the rest of the editorial and design teams at Scholastic UK. And finally to our illustrator Sara Rahmani.

The characters in *Rising After the Fall* are fictional, but they are based on real words from the diaries of Afghan women writers – some of whom are still living in Afghanistan, others are now in different parts of the world. Without their courage this book would not exist.

Thank you all for sharing your stories with us.

Glossary

9/11 – the date in 2001 that al-Qaeda co-ordinated a string of terrorist attacks on American soil. Four planes were hijacked by terrorists; two crashed into the World Trade Center (Twin Towers) in New York, one crashed into the Pentagon in Washington, and the terrorists crashed the final plane into an empty field in Pennsylvania when the passengers fought back. Nearly three thousand people died in these attacks

al-Qaeda – a terrorist organization founded in Peshawar, Pakistan, by Osama bin Laden in 1988 after the Soviet invasion of Afghanistan. The aim of this group is to govern Muslim society under Islamic Sharia Law (*see also* Islamic Sharia Law)

asylum – protection granted to a person fleeing their country in fear of political persecution or human rights violations

bolani – a traditional Afghan flat bread stuffed with potato and leek

Buddhas of Bamyan – ancient twin statues carved into a cliff in the Hazarat region. The Taliban destroyed these in 2001

burqa – a garment Muslim women wear to cover their body and observe modesty

chadari/chador – a garment worn by Muslim women to observe modesty. This garment covers the head and upper body

COVID – an infectious respiratory virus that emerged in 2020 and spread rapidly, causing a global pandemic

election – a system used to vote for a political leader or representative in government

equal rights – when all people have the same rights and protections in laws. These legislations protect people from discrimination and persecution

ethnic group – a community of people tied together by shared ancestry, language, culture or history

fall – as in the 'fall of Kabul'. People say this when referring to when the Taliban retook Kabul and the rest of Afghanistan in August 2021

fraud – manipulating or deceiving a situation for personal gain

gender – the societal, psychological and cultural expressions of men, women and other identities. Gender is not always determined by sex

genocide – the systematic killing of a group or groups of people, often to 'cleanse' a nation of certain ethnic groups

Hazara – an ethnic group of people in Afghanistan and Pakistan

hijab – a head covering worn by Muslim women to observe modesty

human rights – laws and principles designed to protect the bodies, freedoms and liberties of all humans. Human rights include working rights, ethics in war, freedom of speech and many other standards in national and international law

ideology – a set of ideas or beliefs

internally displaced person (IDP) – a person who has been forcibly removed from their home and land but has not left their country

IDP camp – a safe space established to shelter internally displaced persons

Islamic State (IS) – a terrorist group, also known as ISIL (Islamic State of Iraq and the Levant) and ISIS (Islamic State of Syria), and sometimes Daesh. IS was founded in 1999 and gained notoriety in 2014 by managing to occupy many territories in Iraq and Syria. Their power significantly declined in 2017 and they now occupy a markedly smaller amount of territories

Islamic Sharia law – laws that follow the traditions of Islam. Influenced by the Quran and rulings written by religious scholars

Judgement Day – a day in religious books where everybody is resurrected and their sins and good deeds are calculated to determine whether they end up in heaven or hell

minority – a group in a nation that makes up less than half of a population. These groups can be categorized by race, ethnicity, gender identity, religion, sexuality, disability and other identity markers

Mother – young people in Afghanistan sometimes refer to older women as 'Mother' as a term of respect, a bit like 'Madam'

mullah – a religious scholar or leader for Muslims

NATO – the North Atlantic Treaty Organization or NATO is a group of countries from Europe and North America who have agreed to co-operate with one another on political and military matters

Persian Solar Hijri Calendar/Solar Hijri Calendar – an ancient calendar used in Iran and Afghanistan that is based on the observations of Earth's movements around the Sun

prayer beads – religious necklace or bracelet often gripped or rubbed when praying

propaganda – the distribution of information with the aim of swaying public opinion on political matters and agendas

protest – when numerous people co-operate and organize a public expression of disapproval, often to reject a law, idea or political action. Protests can be peaceful or violent

Quran – the holy book of Muslims. The Quran was orally revealed over a period of approximately twenty-three years to the Prophet Muhammad

refugee – a person that has fled their home and crossed international borders in order to escape natural disasters, war, widespread violence or threat of punishment for political or religious beliefs

regime – a strict form of governing a country or region

resilience – having strength in difficult times

segregation – the separation of society on the basis of, for example, race or gender

Shia – Islam has two main sects: Shia and Sunni. Approximately 90% of the world's Muslims are Sunnis. Shia constitute about 10% of all Muslims

social activist – somebody that fights for social justice issues, such as gender equality, animal rights, human rights, workers' rights, etc.

Soviet Union – Union of Soviet Social Republics or the Soviet Union for short, a communist state including Russia and other countries

special forces – a unit in the military that specializes in a certain discipline, such as fighting terrorism

Talib – a member of the Taliban

Taliban – a political movement in Afghanistan that was founded in 1994. The Taliban ruled in Afghanistan from 1996 to 2001 and returned to power in the summer of 2021

terrorism/terrorist – terrorism is a political act of violence with the goal of instilling fear and influencing politics. A terrorist is a person who organizes and commits said acts of violence

tribe – a community of people who share the same language/dialect, history and economic or blood ties

United Nations Assistance Mission in Afghanistan (UNAMA) – a United Nations mission created to assist in uniting the country of Afghanistan, protecting civilians and their human rights. This was formed in 2002 and is based in Kabul, Afghanistan

United Nations High Commission for Refugees (UNHCR) – a global organization created by the UN to work with refugees, asylum seekers and internally displaced people. It was founded by the United Nations in 1950 after many Europeans fled or lost their homes in the Second World War

World Trade Center/Twin Towers – the Twin Towers were buildings located in the financial district of New York, USA. Upon completion, they were the world's tallest buildings

Viersen – a city in Germany

visa – an official document or passport that allows a person to enter, settle in or leave a country for a period of time

Index